Dictionary

BY **Wendell W. Wright**, PH.D.

ASSISTED BY HELENE LAIRD

ILLUSTRATIONS BY Joseph Low

COLLINS WORLD

William Collins+World Publishing Co., Inc.

Published by WM. COLLINS+WORLD PUBLISHING CO., INC.
2080 W. 117th St., Cleveland, Ohio 44111

Library of Congress Cataloging in Publication Data

Wright, Wendell William, 1893-
The rainbow dictionary.
SUMMARY: Defines 2300 words using simple explanations and drawings.
1. English language — Dictionaries, Juvenile.
[1. English language — Dictionaries] I. Laird,, Helene, 1905-
II. Low, Joseph, 1911- III. Title.
PE1628.W87 1978 423 77-89609
ISBN 0-529-05399-3

A	B	C	D	E
F	G	H	I	J
K	L	M	N	O
P	Q	R	S	T
U	V	W	X	Y
		Z		

An Explanation

CHILDREN grow up in a world of bewildering words. From the time they speak their first simple syllables to adulthood, when their vocabulary has increased to thousands of words, their successful adjustment in life is largely dependent, so educators have found, on their knowledge of words. Intellectual growth, broad cultural development, the capacity for expression, and further learning by reading, all come through the assimilation of the meaning of words. A dictionary for children, therefore, is as important a reference book as a dictionary for adults—perhaps even more important. Its scope must naturally be small to keep it within the child's power to absorb and his range of interest, but its construction must be as painstaking and far more imaginative than the construction of the ponderous volumes used by grown-ups.

The Rainbow Dictionary contains 2300 entries, consisting of 2000 main entries and related forms, which children use in speaking and recognize when reading. The words chosen are those that occur most frequently in a consolidation of eight word lists for children from five to eight years old. Five of these word lists are standard published lists; one is from the unpublished research of the author Wendell W. Wright; and two were made expressly for this publication under Mr. Wright's direction. Of the last two, one was based on the most commonly read children's books, the other on an analysis of the comic pages of standard Sunday newspapers sampled over a period of one year.

The vocabulary of *The Rainbow Dictionary* which finally evolved from this extensive research is thus based almost entirely on frequency. This strict adherence to frequency in determining the choice of words was felt to be by far the best and most practical system for a children's dictionary. Consistency of style, in fact, has been disregarded wherever it seemed that to do so would be helpful to the young reader. The parts of verbs given, for instance, are those most frequently used, rather than any regular number of parts chosen merely for the fact that they are, say, the present, past, and future tenses. In some instances four or five parts of a verb will be listed, in others only one or two. The only exception was made in the case of irregular forms, which are all included. In one or two instances the form of the verb given as the main entry is the past tense, because the present tense is very seldom used by the child. The same rule governed the inclusion of plural forms of nouns, and of comparative and superlative forms of adjectives. If children use them frequently, they are entered in the vocabulary; if not, they are omitted. This principle creates a few instances in which the noun appears only in its plural form.

Not only is this vocabulary scheme logical for a child because it follows the working of a child's mind, but it is much simpler for the child because one of the results is that the words are listed in the form in which he is most likely to look them up. *Mouse*, *Goose*, and *Tooth*, for example, are listed as main entries in both singular and plural forms; *Beans* is listed only in the plural form. All irregular plurals of entry words are also listed as main entries in their regular order. Parts of verbs, when entered, follow the main entry as sub-entries; those which are out of alphabetical order are listed again in their proper place as main entries. The one exception to this rule was made for the parts of the verb *to be.* It was felt that the connections between the various and very differently spelled parts of this verb would be difficult for the child to comprehend (as they are for an adult who is not versed in etymology). Therefore, *be*, *am*, *is*, *are*, *was*, *were*, *aren't*, *isn't*, *wasn't*, are each listed as main entries in alphabetical order.

No word has been included which has not been defined in some way. Thus, parts of verbs, plurals of nouns, and comparatives and superlatives of adjectives are treated as fully as main entries, rather than merely listed, and the child has the opportunity of seeing how they are used in relationship to each other. A good example of this type of treatment is found in the word *High:* The yellow dish is high in the cupboard. The white dish is higher. The black dish is the highest of all.

In brief, the object has been to put every word where the child will naturally look for it, to include every word which he will be likely to look for, and to define every word included.

The author has made use of many methods in helping children to learn the meanings of words. The principal methods used are:

1. The picture with its caption—delineating an object, illustrating an action, or illuminating an idea:

    sail—This is a *sail* on a boat.

2. The simple explanation of the meaning of the word:

    navy—A *navy* is all the fighting ships of a country and the men that run them.

3. The use of the word in a sentence with additional facts to help clarify its meaning:

fish—A *fish* lives in the water.

4. The use of the word and a synonymous word or phrase in two otherwise identical sentences. (Synonyms were not used unless they were simpler and more readily understandable to the child than the word being defined, and unless they too were defined in their proper place in the alphabet.)

invite—Patty will *invite* me to her party.
Patty will *ask* me *to come* to her party.

5. The use of the word with its antonym:

clean—Mary's face is *clean.* She washed it. John's face is dirty. He didn't wash it.

6. The use of the word in a quotation:

cow—The friendly *cow* all red and white,
I love with all my heart:
She gives me cream with all her might,
To eat with apple tart.

Very frequently two or three of these ways have been used in defining one word.

The style of language throughout the book is simple; no word is used in the definitions that does not appear in the vocabulary. The expressions are those of children, and the ideas and situations are within the range of the common experience of children.

The pictures by Joseph Low are not only excellent illustrations of the words, they are composed with the skill of a fine artist and the simplicity of a child. In them are combined imagination, freshness, vivacity, joyousness. They are not without a touch of the exotic which so appeals to children. Most of the situations depicted in the drawings are taken out of the experiences of children, and an effort has been made to draw upon the gay and happy experiences of children in most cases. There are over 1100 pictures in this book.

The quotations have been carefully selected from the children's favorites: Mother Goose, Robert Louis Stevenson, Lewis Carroll, and others—not only to illustrate the word, but to add interest and playfulness to a book which must not be dull lest it fail its purpose.

The Rainbow Dictionary, then, is a picture book and a book of knowledge, but above all, a book of words and their meanings.

THE PUBLISHERS

A a

A a I have **a** ball.

I have **one** ball.

able Robert **is able** to read.

Robert **can** read.

aboard

Daddy got **aboard** a train to go to New York.

Daddy got **on** a train to go to New York. Then he went aboard a big ship.

about I will tell you a story **about** my dog.

John is **about** as tall as Jim.

John is **almost** as tall as Jim.

The wind blows the leaves **about** the streets.

The wind blows the leaves **around** the streets.

above

The rooster is **above** the dog.
The rooster is **higher than** the dog.

Here the dog is above the rooster.

---

absent

I was **absent** from school today.
I was **not at** school today. I was **not there.**

---

accident

I dropped the cup on the floor. I did not mean to drop it. It was an **accident.**

A truck ran into our automobile and broke the wheel. It was an accident.

---

ache

I have an **ache** in my shoulder.
I have a **pain** in my shoulder.

My ear **aches.**
My ear **hurts.**

---

across

The boys walked **across** the street.
The boys walked **from one side** of the street **to the other side.**

act

Jack is going to **act** like a clown.

Jack is going to **play** he is a clown.

If Bobby is tired, he will **act** like a bad boy.

If Bobby is tired, he will **behave** like a bad boy.

acted Judy **acted** like a good girl in kindergarten this morning.

acting I am **acting** the part of a fairy in our school play.

---

add If you **add** one and one, you have two.

If you **put together** one and one, you have two.

This sign + means add. 1 + 1 = 2.

You must **add** sugar to make your cocoa sweet.

You must **put in** sugar to make your cocoa sweet.

added When I **added** two and two, I got four. That was the right answer.

---

address Write your name and **address.**

Write your name and **the place where you live.**

John told us his name and his address

John Mills
45 Ash Street
Kent, Ohio 44240

---

afraid

The cat is **afraid** of the dog.

The cat is **scared** of the dog.

after

The girl is running **after** the dog. The girl is running **behind** the dog. She is trying to catch him.

Here the dog is running after the girl.

I came home **after** you did.

I came home **later than** you did.

---

afternoon **After twelve o'clock noon** is **afternoon.** The sun is in the west in the afternoon. The sun is in the east in the morning. I am going to play with Jane this afternoon.

---

afterward I am going to the store now, but **afterward** we can go swimming.

I am going to the store now, but **later** we can go swimming.

When I first got my dog, he was a little puppy. Afterward he was a big dog.

---

again Read the story **again.**

Read the story **one more time.**

against Bob pushed **against** the gate. He tried to push the gate open.

Alice leaned against the tree.

Sam and Harry played **against** each other in the baseball game.

Sam and Harry played **on different sides** in the baseball game.

---

age What is your **age**, Bill?

How old are you, Bill? I am six years old. My age is six years.

---

ago The Bible was written long **ago.**

The Bible was written long **before now.**

Mother went to the store five minutes ago. She went five minutes before now.

---

agree The boy and girl **agree.**

The boy and girl **think alike.**

Will John **agree** to do it?

Will John **be willing** to do it?

Too much candy will not **agree with** me.

Too much candy will not **be good for** me.

agreed Arthur said it was very cold. Joe **agreed** with him. Joe **also thought** it was cold.

ahead

The boy is **ahead** of the girl.
The boy is **in front** of the girl.

Here the girl is ahead of the boy.

---

air We live in the **air.** Fish live in the water. We breathe air. The airplane flies through the air. We blow air into our balloons. Father puts air into his auto tires.

---

airplane

An **airplane** is a **machine that flies.** There are many different kinds of **airplanes.**

---

airport

Airplanes land and take off at an **airport.** My daddy landed at the airport today in an airplane.

---

alarm The **alarm** clock has a bell that rings. It helps us wake up on time. A fire alarm calls the firemen to a fire.

If you scream suddenly, you will **alarm** your mother.
If you scream suddenly, you will **scare** your mother.

album One kind of **album** is a book with empty pages in it. We can paste pictures or stamps in an album. Or an album may be a book for holding records.

---

alike

These twin girls look very much **alike.**
These twin girls look very much **the same.**
They are dressed alike.

---

alive

This plant is **alive.**

This plant is dead.

---

all

All of this cake is here.
Every bit of this cake is here.

This cake is not all here. Part of this cake is gone.

I gave Don **all** of my marbles.
I gave Don **every one** of my marbles.

---

alligator Did you ever see an **alligator** at the zoo? Alligators live in rivers in the warm part of our country. They live in many other countries, too.

allow I will **allow** Nancy to ride the pony.
I will **let** Nancy ride the pony.

allowed Daddy **allowed** my dog to ride in the car.

---

almost

Mary is **almost** as tall as her mother.

Mary is **nearly** as tall as her mother.

---

alone Philip does not cry when he is **alone.**
Philip does not cry when he is **not with anyone.**

Can you dress yourself **alone?**
Can you dress yourself **without anyone to help?**

---

along The cat is walking **along** the fence.
John is walking along the street.

When Mother takes a walk, I like to go **along.** I beg her to take me with her.

---

aloud When we talk, we speak **aloud.** When we whisper, we do not speak aloud. The children may not speak aloud in the library. They must speak in a soft voice.

---

already Peter has learned to read **already.**
Peter has learned to read **before this time.**

I have my dolls in the playhouse **already.**
I have my dolls in the playhouse **by this time.**

also

Jerry has a ball.

Baby has a ball **also.**
Baby has a ball **too.**

---

although We went to the picnic **although** it was raining.
We went to the picnic **even though** it was raining.
John walked to school although he liked to ride his bicycle.

---

always When the sun shines, it is **always** light.
When the sun shines, it is **at all times** light.

---

am I **am** sleepy. I am going to bed.

America

This map shows North **America** and South America. The United States is part of North America. The United States is sometimes called America.

American I am an **American.** The people of the United States are called **Americans.** Sometimes all the people who live in North and South America are called Americans.

The **American** flag is red, white, and blue.

among Some weeds were **among** the flowers in our garden.

Some weeds were **mixed with** the flowers in our garden.

Mother divided the candy **among** the boys. She gave some to each of them.

---

an Mother put **an** egg and an onion on the kitchen table.

Mother put **one** egg and one onion on the kitchen table.

---

and One **and** one make two.

I will eat dinner and then go to bed.

---

angry

This man is **angry**. This man is happy.

Sometimes when we are angry we say, "I'm mad."

---

animal

The rabbit is an **animal.** The squirrel is an animal too. **Animals** are alive. They can move and breathe and eat. They can have baby animals. You see wild animals in the zoo. You see tame animals in the barnyard.

Wild Animals

Tame Animals

ankle

My **ankle** is the part of my body between my foot and my leg.

---

another Fred broke his ball bat.

He had to get **another.**

He had to get **a different one.**

Mary had one cooky.

Mother gave her **another.**

Mother gave her **one more.**

Sally and Jim like one **another.** Sally likes Jim, and Jim likes Sally.

---

answer How much is two and two? The right **answer** is four.

James did not **answer** when his mother called.

Ellen will **answer** the telephone when it rings.

answered Bill asked me a question, and **I answered.**

---

ant An **ant** is **one kind of bug.**

These are **ants.**

any You may have **any** flower from the garden.

You may have **one** flower **that you choose** from the garden.

Have you **any** old papers to give away?

Have you **some** old papers to give away?

---

anybody Did **anybody** see my dog?

Did **any person** see my dog?

Did **anyone** see my dog?

---

anyone May **anyone** come to the show?

May **any person** come to the show?

May **anybody** come to the show?

---

anything

You may have **anything** from this table.

You may have **any one of the things** from this table.

Carol's new dress isn't **anything** like mine.

Carol's new dress isn't **at all** like mine.

---

anyway My mother cannot take me to the party, but I am going **anyway.**

---

anywhere I will go **anywhere** you go.

I will go **any place** you go.

apartment

An **apartment** house is a building where many families live. Our apartment has four rooms. It is on the first floor of this apartment house.

---

appear In the spring the leaves **appear** on the trees.

In the spring the leaves **come out** on the trees.

In a minute the mailman will **appear.**

In a minute the mailman will **come where he can be seen.**

---

apple

An **apple** is a fruit. Mother makes good apple pies.

Apples grow on trees. The farmer picks the apples and puts them in baskets to sell.

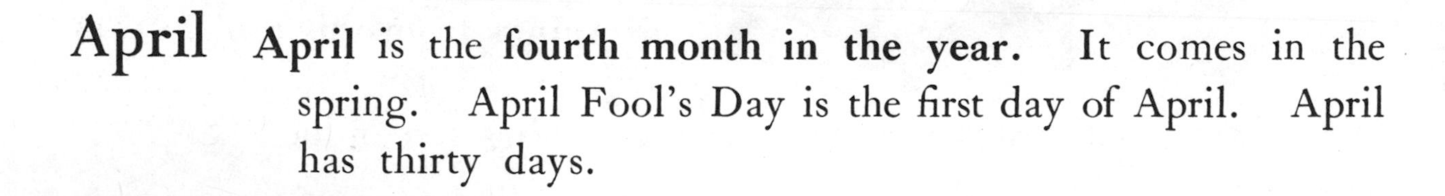

April **April** is the **fourth month in the year.** It comes in the spring. April Fool's Day is the first day of April. April has thirty days.

---

apron

Mother is putting on her **apron.** The apron keeps her dress clean.

are Billy and **I are** happy today because we are going swimming. We are going right now.

When we say, "How are you?" we mean, "How do you feel?"

---

aren't **Aren't** means **are not.**

We aren't going downtown till this afternoon.

We are not going downtown till this afternoon.

---

arm

Jerry has a strong **arm.**

One of these chairs has **arms,** but the other has no arms.

---

army Many men are in the **army** when we have a war. Men fight for our country when they are in the army. A man in the army is called a soldier. Jimmy's father was an aviator in the army.

---

around

Nancy has a ribbon **around** her head.

When mother hugs me, she puts her arms around me.

The dog ran around and around the tree.

arrive Mother has been away, but she is coming home.
She will **arrive** tomorrow.
She will **come** tomorrow.

---

arrow

This pointed stick is an **arrow.**

Jim has a bow and arrow. Indians hunted with a bow and arrow.

---

as

George is **as** tall as his father.

We might **as** well wait until it stops raining.

Richard acts **as** if he had a secret.

---

ask Mary wants a cooky. She will **ask** her mother for it.
When I **ask** my teacher a question, she tells me the answer.

---

asleep

This child is **asleep.**

---

astronaut An **astronaut** flies way out in space in a machine called a **rocket. Astronauts** can fly to the moon.

---

at The children are **at** the farm today. Tomorrow they will be at school.

Dan and Bill are throwing snowballs **at** each other.

ate Kitty **ate** all his food.
His plate is empty.

---

atom **Atoms** are the tiny bits that all things are made of. Atoms are so small you cannot see them. But this picture shows how we think an atom might look if it were this big.

---

attention You must pay **attention** while I show you how to write. You must listen and watch carefully.

When the captain wants the soldiers to stand straight, he says, "**Attention!**"

---

attic

This house has an **attic.** The wall has been taken away so that you can see into the attic. The children go upstairs to the attic under the roof to play.

August **August** is the **eighth month of the year.** It comes in the summer. There are thirty-one days in August.

---

aunt My **father's sister** is my **aunt.** My **mother's sister** is my **aunt.** My **uncle's wife** is my **aunt,** too.

---

auto **Auto** is a short word for **automobile.**
We rode to town in the auto.

automobile

Daddy takes me for a ride in his **automobile.**

A jeep is a kind of automobile.

Trucks are **automobiles,** too.

---

autumn **Autumn** is one of the four seasons of the year. Between summer and winter we have autumn. **Autumn** is also called **fall.** In the autumn the leaves fall from some trees.

---

aviator An **aviator** is a person who flies an airplane. My father was an aviator in the war.

---

awake Bess is **awake** now.
Bess is **not asleep** now.

---

away The boy ran **away.**
The boy ran **from that place.**

---

awhile Let us wait here **awhile.** Let us wait here **a short time.** We waited awhile for the bus.

---

ax This is an **ax.**

George Washington chopped down the cherry tree with an ax.

B b

babies Twin **babies** live next door to us.

It is a nice spring day. The mothers have taken their babies out to the park.

baby 

We all love the **baby**.

back Tommy rides on Daddy's **back**.

There is dry glue on the **back** of a stamp.

Jack gave Sally a penny. Now he wants it **back**.

Mother went to the store. Then she came **back**.

Father **backs** the car out.

Bb

backward David fell **backward** off the stool.

He **fell on his back.**

Can you walk backward?

Bob can count backward. He counts 5, 4, 3, 2, 1.

When we count forward, we say 1, 2, 3, 4, 5.

---

bad The **bad** monkey stole a banana.

The **naughty** monkey stole a banana.

Too much candy is **bad** for you.

Too much candy is **not good** for you. It will make you sick.

---

bag Here is a **bag** for traveling and a bag for shopping. The other bag is Mother's purse.

---

baggage

These trunks and bags are **baggage.** We carry clothes and other things in them when we travel.

---

bake Mother can **bake** a loaf of bread.

Mother can **cook** a loaf of bread **in the oven.**

baked At the picnic the boys **baked** potatoes in a fire.

baking Mother is **baking** cookies today. She is baking a pie, too.

baker

The **baker** makes bread, cake, and cookies. He bakes them in big ovens. We buy them at the store.

The butcher, the baker, the candlestick maker,
They all went to sea in a tub.

---

bakery

The bread we buy at the store is baked at the **bakery.** Cakes and cookies are made at the bakery.

---

ball

We throw the **ball.** The ball bounces.
Most balls are round.
A football is not round.

---

balloon

I have a blue **balloon.**

These **balloons** are filled with air.

---

banana

A **banana** is a fruit.

It is good to eat. Here are many **bananas.** They grow in a bunch like this. The bunches of bananas grow on a tree.

band

These men playing music are a **band.**

A rubber **band** holds papers together.

---

bang

The guns go **bang, bang.** They make a loud noise.

---

bank

A **bank** is a **place to keep money.**

I keep my pennies in a piggy bank.

My dad keeps his money in a bank downtown. It is a big building.

The **land at the edge of a river** is called the **bank** of the river.

---

bare

The cupboard was **bare.**

The cupboard was **empty.**

Old Mother Hubbard went to the cupboard
To get her poor dog a bone,
But when she got there the cupboard was bare,
And so the poor dog had none.

Jerry's feet were **bare** when he took off his shoes and socks.

bark A dog can **bark.** A seal can bark, too.

The **bark** of a tree is the part on the outside. It is like a coat for the tree.

---

barn The farmer keeps his horses and cows in the **barn.** He puts food for the animals in the barn.

---

barrel

This is a **barrel.** When we moved, my mother packed her dishes in a barrel.

---

baseball

These children are playing **baseball.** Baseball is a game.

A **baseball** is also one kind of ball.

---

basement The **lowest part of a building** is sometimes called the **basement.** The basement is usually partly below the ground. The basement is often called the cellar. Not every house has a basement.

Bb

basket

We put our Easter eggs in a **basket.** My mother brought home her groceries in a basket.

---

basketball We saw two teams play a game of **basketball.**

The ball they played with is called a **basketball.**

---

bat

The ball is hit with a **bat** in baseball.

A **bat** is a furry little animal that can fly. It has wings, but it is not a bird. It looks like a mouse with wings.

---

bath The boy takes a **bath.**

bathroom The bathtub is in the **bathroom.**

bathtub The boy is in the **bathtub.**

---

be Will you **be** at school tomorrow? Yes, I will be there.

I shall be six years old next week.

"Be good," says Mother.

been Mother says Baby has **been** good today.

being When you are **being** good, you are doing what is right.

beach  A **beach** is the **sandy land at the edge of the water.**

We went swimming and then played on the beach.

---

bead 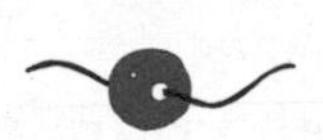 This is a **bead.**

Mother is wearing a string of **beads** around her neck.

---

beans **Beans** are a vegetable. String beans grow in the garden. We had a dish of baked beans at dinner.

---

bear A **bear** is a wild animal. Did you ever see **bears** at the zoo? Did you ever see dancing bears at the circus?

---

beard  This old man has a long **beard.**

This old man has long **hair growing on his face.**

Daddy shaves his beard every day.

---

beast A **beast** is an animal. When you go to the zoo, you hear the wild **beasts** roaring.

beat See the boy **beat** the drum.

See the boy **strike** the drum.

Can you **beat** him in the race?

Can you **win from** him in the race?

Mother will **beat** the eggs.

Did you ever feel your heart **beat?**

---

beautiful My mother is **beautiful.**

My mother is **very nice to look at.**

The music was **beautiful.**

The music was **very nice to hear.**

---

became The seed **became** a plant.

The seed **grew into** a plant.

What **became** of my new doll? Where can it be?

---

because Why is John wet? He is wet **because** he fell in the water.

---

bed

I sleep in my **bed.**

Mother has a **bed** of flowers in her garden.

These are **beds** of flowers in a park.

bedroom The **bedroom** is a **room for sleeping.** My bed is in the bedroom.

---

bedtime Betty's **bedtime** is eight o'clock.

Betty's **time to go to bed** is eight o'clock.

---

bee  This is a **bee.** The bee buzzes.

Bees live in a little house called a hive.

Bees store honey in their hives.

---

beef We like to eat **beef.** It is the meat from cattle. We had roast beef for dinner.

---

been Mother says Baby has **been** good today.

Pussy cat, pussy cat, where have you been?
I've been to London to look at the queen.

---

beet A **beet** is a plant that grows in the garden. It is a vegetable. We eat the dark red root of the beet. Mother cooked **beets** for dinner.

---

before The children play games **before** school starts.

The children play games **earlier than** school starts.

The dog went **before** us.

The dog went **in front of** us.

beg I **beg** my mother for a piece of candy. I want the candy very much.

See my dog sit up and **beg** for the ball. He wants me to give it to him.

begged My dog sat up and **begged** for the ball.

My little sister **begged** me to play school with her.

---

began Yesterday Baby **began** to walk.

Yesterday Baby **started** to walk.

---

begin Now I will **begin** to make a picture.

Now I will **start** to make a picture.

began Yesterday Baby **began** to walk.

---

behave I told my naughty dog to **behave.**

I told my naughty dog to **act well.**

My brother is **behaving** like a clown.

My brother is **acting** like a clown.

---

behind James stands **behind** Martha in line.

James stands **in back of** Martha in line.

Jean is peeping from behind the tree.

being When you are **being** good, you are doing what is right.

---

believe I **believe** that story.

I **think** that story **is true.**

---

bell

The **bell** rings.

Ding, dong, bell,
Pussy's in the well.

People ring our door bell when they come to visit us.

The **bells** in the churches rang to tell us to come to church.

---

belong Does the ball **belong** to Baby? Yes, it is Baby's ball.

---

below The floor is **below** the ceiling. The ceiling is above the floor.

---

belt

Father wears a **belt** on his trousers. Mother wears a pretty red belt on her white dress.

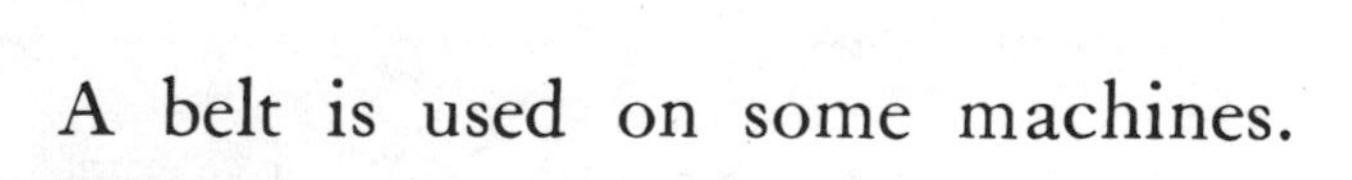

A belt is used on some machines.

---

bench

My father has a **bench** in the basement. He works on it when he makes things. It is his workbench.

Two people are sitting on this **bench.**

bend He had to **bend** the bow to shoot the arrow.

Can you **bend** down and touch the floor?

There was a **bend** in the road.

---

beneath

The cat is **beneath** the table.

The cat is **under** the table. The hat and gloves are on the table.

---

berries **Berries** are a small juicy fruit. There are many kinds of berries. I like to eat blackberries, strawberries, and raspberries.

---

berry

What kind of **berry** is this? It is a strawberry.

---

beside George sits **beside** Mother at the table.

George sits **next to** Mother at the table.

I put the red book **beside** the green one.

I put the red book **close to** the green one.

besides Robert got an electric train for Christmas, **besides** books and other presents.

Orange juice is good for me; **besides,** I like it.

---

best I like candy, cake, and ice cream, but I like ice cream **best.**

I like candy, cake, and ice cream, but I like ice cream **most.**

Sarah's writing is the **best** in the room. No one else in the room writes as well as Sarah.

---

better Ted's writing is **better** than Mary's. Mary's writing is not as good as Ted's.

Carol was sick yesterday, but today she feels **better.**

Carol was sick yesterday, but today she feels **not so sick.**

Peter had the measles last month. Now he is **better.** He is well.

---

between

This apple is **between** two books. This apple has a book on each side of it.

---

beyond

The town is **beyond** the hill.

The town is **farther away than** the hill.

We can see all of the town after we climb the hill.

bib Baby wears a **bib** when she eats. The bib keeps her dress clean.

Bible

This is a **Bible.** The Bible was written long ago. The Bible is a book that is read in church.

---

bicycle

Johnny got a **bicycle** for his birthday. He likes to ride his bicycle.

---

big The bear is **big.**

The bear is **large.**

The bird is little.

Have you read the story about The Three Bears?

bigger The mother bear is **bigger** than the baby bear.

biggest The father bear is the **biggest** of the three.

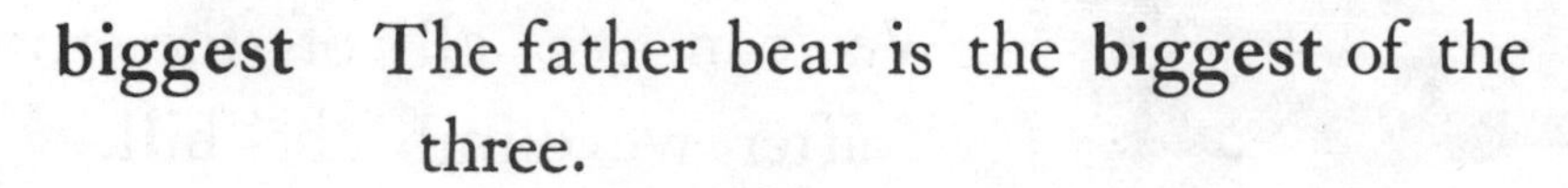

bill

The duck has a bug in his **bill.** A bird's bill is his mouth.

Oh, what a queer bird is the pelican!
His bill holds more than his belly can.

My mother bought a new dress. She did not pay for it when she bought it. Later the store sent her a **bill** for it. The bill is a paper that tells how much she must pay.

A dollar **bill** is money. My aunt gave me a dollar bill for my birthday. I bought a new toy with my dollar bill.

bird A **bird** has wings. A bird has feathers, too. Most **birds** can fly. There are many kinds of birds.

birdhouse

We have a **birdhouse** in our yard.

We have a little **house for the birds** in our yard.

---

birthday I am seven years old today. It is my **birthday.** I was born on this day of this month seven years ago.

---

bit Mary used a **bit** of cloth to make a doll dress.

Mary used a **small piece** of cloth to make a doll dress.

I **bit** into my sandwich.

---

bite Mary took a big **bite** of the cake. The bite was as much as she could take in her mouth at one time.

The dog can **bite** the stick.

The dog can **cut into** the stick **with his teeth.**

bit I **bit** into my sandwich.

bites Baby **bites** the spoon.

---

bitter Some things taste **bitter.** The outside part of an orange tastes bitter.

---

black

Black is a color. Many people of the world have a skin color from light brown to very dark. They are called **black** people.

blackberry The **blackberry** is a small fruit that grows on a bush. The blackberry is not really black. It is dark purple. Mother baked a blackberry pie.

---

blackbird We saw a **blackbird** today. The blackbird was black with some red on its wings.

---

blackboard

My teacher writes on the **blackboard** at school. Joyce draws a picture on the blackboard.

---

blame Do you **blame** me because the sled turned over? Do you think it was my fault? I was not to blame. It was not my fault.

---

blanket I have a **blanket** on my bed to keep me warm. In winter the snow is like a blanket on the ground.

---

blaze When wood burns, it makes a **blaze.**
When wood burns, it makes a **flame.**

blew When **I** turned the fan on it **blew** in my face.
It **made air move** against my face.

The wind blew the clothes on the line.

When **I blew** the horn, it made a noise.

Daddy **blew up** my balloon.

Daddy **put air into** my balloon.

---

blind **Blind** persons are sometimes led by guide dogs.

They **cannot see** and the dogs help them find their way.

---

block

My father works in a store in this **block.**

What are you able to build with your blocks?
Castles and palaces, temples and docks.
Rain may keep raining and others go roam,
But I can be happy and building at home.

We play with **blocks** like these.

bloom When a plant has flowers, we say it is in **bloom.** This plant is in bloom.

Many plants **bloom** in the spring.

Many plants **have flowers** in the spring.

blooming Some of the bushes in our yard are **blooming.**

---

blossom The flower of a tree is called a **blossom.**

The apple tree is in **blossom.**

The apple tree is in **bloom.**

---

blow I will turn the fan on. It will **blow** in my face.

It will **make air move** against my face.

When you **blow** a horn, it makes a noise.

Daddy will **blow up** my balloon.

Daddy will **put air into** my balloon.

blew The wind **blew** the clothes on the line.

blowing Our teacher is **blowing** her whistle for the game to start.

blows The wind **blows** the leaves.

---

blue

This is the color **blue.**

The boy's suit is blue.

bluebird The **bluebird** has blue wings and back. He has an orange breast. The bluebird can sing.

---

board A **board** is a flat piece of wood cut from a log. A board used to be a part of a tree.

---

boat A **boat** carries us over the water. A large boat is called a ship. One of these **boats** is a sailboat. One is a rowboat. Do you know which is which?

---

body George has a strong, healthy **body.** All the parts of a human being or an animal are its body.

---

boil When we make water or milk hot enough, it will **boil.** See the water boil and the steam come from it. One way to cook food is to boil it.

boiled My mother **boiled** Daddy's breakfast eggs for three minutes.

---

bone

My dog likes to chew a **bone.**

Animals have **bones** in their bodies. People have bones, too.

book Bill has a **book.** It is fun to read a book. Jack and Sally like to read **books.** Some books have pictures in them.

---

boot A **boot** is a **kind of shoe.** It covers the foot and a part of the leg. There are several kinds of **boots.** We wear boots in the snow. We wear boots when we ride horses.

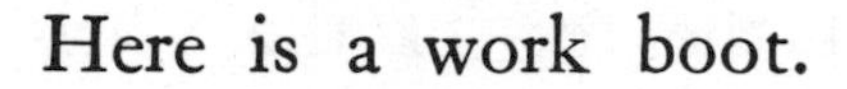

Here is a work boot.

Here is a riding boot.

---

born We have some new kittens at our house. They were **born** last week.

---

borrow When a playmate **borrows** something from me, I expect to get it back again. My playmate gets to use it for a while, but should return it. Jane **borrowed** my bicycle last week. I'm going to ask her for it.

---

both The boy and girl are **both** riding in the car. **The two of them** are riding in the car. I covered both my ears with my cap.

bother My dog's barking does not **bother** me because I know he is having fun. But when my little brother cries, it does bother me. I think he may be hurt.

We did not **bother** to look for the lost ball.

We did not **take the trouble** to look for the lost ball.

---

bottle

A **bottle** for baby's milk.

A bottle for medicine.

Most **bottles** are made of glass.

---

bottom

The presents are at the **bottom** of the Christmas tree. The star is at the top of the Christmas tree. The bottom of my shoe is leather.

Dad paints the bottom of his boat every summer.

---

bought I **bought** a pencil for five cents.

I **paid** five cents **and got** a pencil.

---

bounce

I can **bounce** the ball twenty-five times without missing. When I bounce the ball, it jumps up and down.

bounces The ball **bounces** because it is made of rubber.

bow 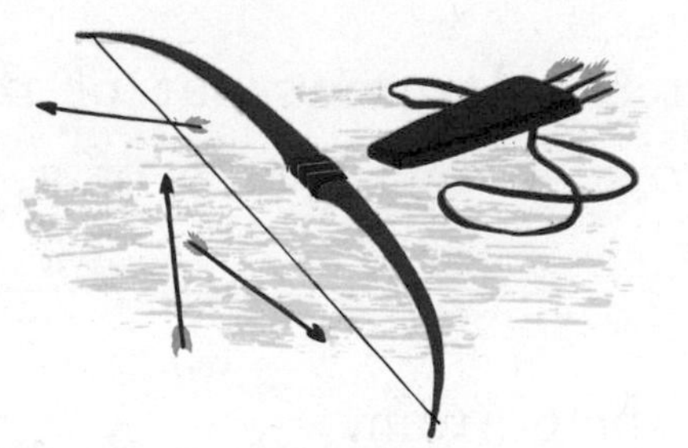 This is a **bow** and arrows.

Sally has a ribbon **bow** in her hair.

She is making a **bow**.

---

bow'wow "**Bow-wow,**" says the dog. He is barking.

---

bowl A **bowl** is a deep, round dish.

Old King Cole was a merry old soul;
A merry old soul was he.
He called for his pipe and he called for his bowl
And he called for his fiddlers three.

---

box Georgie keeps his toys in a **box.**
Mother buys cookies in a box.
Joe made a dog house from a big box.

---

boxes We used three **boxes** for chairs in our playhouse.

---

boy A **boy** grows up to be a man.
We have a new baby boy in our family.
There are nine **boys** on our baseball team.

branch A **branch** is a part of a tree. It grows out of the trunk of the tree. Leaves grow on the branch of a tree.

---

branches The trunk of a tree is at the bottom. The **branches** are at the top of the tree. Birds sit on the branches of the tree.

---

brave Firemen are **brave.**

Firemen are **not afraid.**

---

bread

This is a loaf of **bread.** Bread is made from flour. I like bread and butter. I like bread and jelly, too.

---

break Sue dropped the dish. Did it **break?**

Did it **come apart into pieces?**

If you want to be healthy, you must not **break** the rule: "Early to bed."

If you want to be healthy, you must not **act against** the rule: "Early to bed."

broke George **broke** his new baseball bat.

broken Some of the branches have been **broken** off the tree by the wind.

breakfast **Breakfast** is the first meal of the day. I eat my breakfast before I go to school.

---

breast

The pilot wears silver wings on his **breast.** The robin has a red breast. When Baby goes to sleep, she puts her head on Mother's breast.

---

breath Your **breath** is the **air you breathe in and out.** When you blow your breath on your hands in winter, it feels warm. You blow your breath into a balloon when you blow it up.

---

breathe I **breathe** very fast after I have been running.

I **take in and let out air** very fast after I have been running.

I breathe through my nose.

---

breeze A **breeze** is a **little wind.** The breeze blows the leaves on the trees.

The electric fan makes a breeze.

---

brick

A **brick** is made from clay.
It is baked in a hot oven.

The man is making a wall of **bricks.**

bridge

This is a **bridge.** The bridge is over the water. We cross over the river on the bridge.

---

bright Sunshine is **bright** during the day. The lights are bright at night. Red is a bright color.

Bill is a **bright** boy. He learns things easily.

---

bring Patty can **bring** the books to Mother.

Patty can **carry** the books to Mother.

Will you **bring** your sister when you come to play?

Will you **take** your sister **with you** when you come to play?

bringing Jim is **bringing** me a toy from the city.

brought Alice **brought** a friend to kindergarten with her.

---

broadcast We listened to a **broadcast** over the radio.

---

broil We like meat when it is **broiled.**

We like meat when it is **cooked close to a flame.**

Our family is having a picnic in the backyard. We will all **broil** some hamburgers made from ground meat. We will **broil** them on the grill.

broke George **broke** his new baseball bat. It **came apart** into two pieces.

Susan **broke** the rule: "Early to bed."

Susan **acted against** the rule: "Early to bed."

---

broken

Some of the branches have been **broken** off the tree by the wind.

---

broom We sweep up the dirt with a **broom.** We swept the leaves off the walk with a broom.

---

brother Mother and Father have two children, Jane and Tom. I am Jane. Tom is my **brother.** Two boys live in the house next door. They are **brothers.** They have the same mother and father.

---

brought Mother **brought** my lunch to me in bed.

Mother **carried** my lunch to me in bed.

---

brown

This is the color **brown.**

This shoe is brown.

brush The man paints the picture with a small paint **brush.** We paint our house with a large paint **brush.**

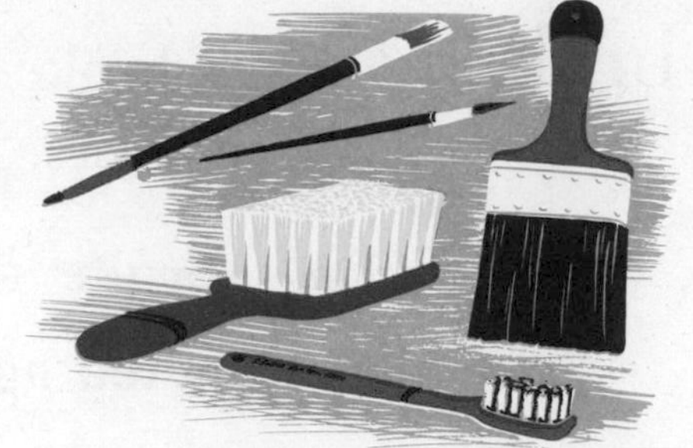

I **brush** my teeth with a tooth brush. I brush my hair with a hair brush.

brushed

Daddy **brushed** his coat.

Daddy **cleaned the dust off** his coat **with a brush.**

---

bucket

I can carry water in a **bucket.**

I can carry water in a **pail.**

---

bug A **bug** has legs. Sometimes it has wings, too. Here are three **bugs.** Some bugs crawl. Some bugs hop. Some bugs fly.

---

buggy Baby rides in a baby **buggy.** Mother pushes it.

Baby rides in a baby **carriage.**

---

build Peggy can **build** a doll's house of blocks.

Peggy can **put together** a doll's house of blocks.

built Uncle Harry **built** a dog house in the yard for Spot.

building Our store is a **building.** A house is a building. There are many different kinds of **buildings.** Find another building in this picture.

built Uncle Harry **built** a dog house in the yard for Spot.

Uncle Harry **put together** a dog house in the yard for Spot.

---

bumblebee A **bumblebee** is a **large bee that makes a buzz.** Have you ever seen **bumblebees** flying among the flowers?

---

bump I fell down and my head hit the floor.

I have a **bump** on my head.

I have a **swelled place** on my head.

Don't ride your tricycle in the house. You may **bump** the chairs.

You may **hit** the chairs.

bumped I **bumped** my elbow on the desk.

---

bun A **bun** is like a very small loaf of bread. We made a sandwich with a bun and some meat.

---

bunch We put flowers together to make a **bunch** of flowers.

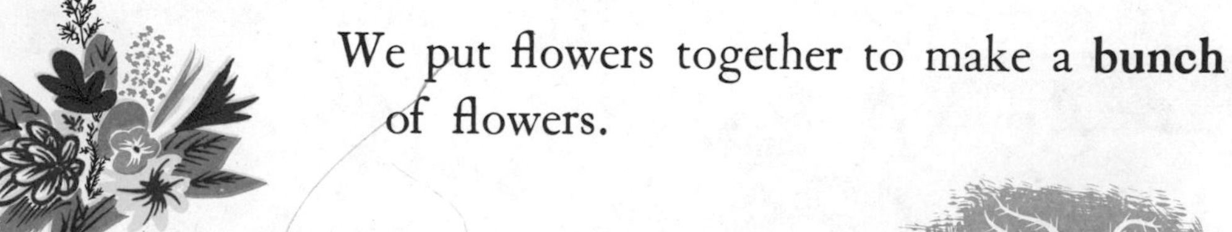

Here is a bunch of radishes.

bundle

The boy carries a heavy **bundle.**

The boy carries a heavy **package.**

Many things tied or wrapped together are a bundle.

Mother says, "**Bundle up** before going outdoors."

Mother says, "**Dress in warm clothes** before going outdoors."

---

bunny We call our pet rabbit a **bunny.** Our bunny has long ears and a very short tail.

---

burn We **burn** wood in our fireplace.

burned We **burned** some dead leaves in the fire. I burned my fingers on a hot iron.

burning The house was **burning.** The firemen came to put out the fire with water.

burns Our stove **burns** gas.

---

bury We decided to **bury** our kitty when she died. We dug a deep hole in the yard. We put her in it and covered her with the earth.

---

bus

A **bus** is a **large automobile with many seats.** We ride to school on the bus. Daddy rides to work on the bus.

bush

This is a **bush.** A bush is smaller than a tree.

Here we go round the mulberry bush,
The mulberry bush, the mulberry bush,
Here we go round the mulberry bush,
So early in the morning.

---

bushes There are many **bushes** in our yard. Most trees are larger than bushes.

---

busy John is a very **busy** boy.
John is a very **active** boy.

Mother was **busy** all day.
Mother was **working** all day.

---

but He ran fast, **but** he could not catch the dog.
He ran fast, **yet** he could not catch the dog.

There is no one in the yard **but** me.
There is no one in the yard **except** me.

---

butcher

The **butcher** cuts up meat for us. We buy meat from the butcher.

butter We make **butter** from milk. Butter tastes good on our bread.
Mary bought a pound of butter.

---

buttercup A **buttercup** is a plant with a bright yellow flower. Its flower looks like a cup.

---

butterflies The wings of **butterflies** are pretty.

---

butterfly

This is a **butterfly**. A butterfly has four large wings and a tiny body.

---

button

Mother will **button** my coat before I go outdoors.

I sew a **button** on my doll's dress.

Did you ever play "Button, Button, Who's Got the Button"?

I have six buttons on my coat.

These are **buttons**.

buy To **buy** is to **give money and get something for it.** I buy a top for ten cents.

bought I **bought** a pencil for five cents.
I **paid** five cents **and got** a pencil.

---

buzz The bee says, "**Buzz, buzz.**"

---

by The dog lies **by** the boy.
The dog lies **near** the boy.

I'll be there **by** five o'clock.
I'll be there **not later than** five o'clock.

I made my doll dress **by** hand.
I made my doll dress **with** my hands.

We went to the swimming hole **by** the path.
We went to the swimming hole **along** the path.

C c

cabbage

Cabbage is a vegetable. Its leaves grow in a large, tight ball. We call this ball a head of cabbage.

cabin

In summer we live in a **cabin** at the lake. Our cabin is built of logs.

cage

We have a bird in a **cage** at our house. Monkeys at the zoo are kept in a cage.

cake

Mother baked a **cake** for my birthday.

A **piece of soap** is called a **cake** of soap.

calendar A **calendar** shows the days and the months of the year.

---

calf A **calf** is a **baby cow.**

---

call Mother will **call,** "Children, come to lunch."
Mother will **say loudly,** "Children, come to lunch."

Did you **call** Patty on the telephone?
Did you **talk to** Patty on the telephone?

My name is Richard, but my friends **call** me Dick.
My name is Richard, but my friends **name** me Dick.

Aunt Susan came to **call on** us.
Aunt Susan came to **visit** us.

called I **called** to my dog, "Spot! Here Spot! Come here!"

calling He heard me **calling** and came to me.

---

came All the birds **came** to the wedding of Jenny Wren and Cock Robin.

---

camel

The **camel** is an animal with a hump on its back. Sometimes a camel has two humps. A man can ride on a camel.

camp This boy is living in a **camp.**
Soldiers live in an army camp.

can

In this picture is a milk **can,** a can of fruit, and an ash can. Can you tell which is which?

I **can** pull myself up.
I **am able to** pull myself up.

could Jane **could** jump the rope.

Canada

Canada is a country in North America.
The United States and Canada are neighbors.

candle

The **candle** makes a pretty light when it burns.

Jack be nimble, Jack be quick,
Jack jump over the candlestick.

I am six years old today. There are six **candles** on my birthday cake.

candy Do you like **candy?** Most candy is made of sugar. Candy is sweet.

cane Grandpa always carries a **cane.**
Grandpa always carries a **stick to help him walk.**

---

cannot Baby **cannot** walk yet.
Baby **is not able** to walk yet.

---

canoe

A **canoe** is a small, light boat. I like to ride in a canoe on the water. We went across the lake in the canoe.

---

can't **Can't** means **cannot.** I can't ride a bicycle yet.

---

cap

Johnny has a new **cap.** He wears his cap on his head.

Put a **cap** on the bottle.
Put a **cover** on the bottle.

---

captain A **captain** is a leader. This captain is the leader of an army company. All the soldiers of his company must do as he says.

This man is captain of a ship. All the sailors on a ship must obey the captain.

car

An automobile is one kind of **car.**

People ride in cars on streets and roads.

This is a freight car on a train. There were twenty **cars** in the freight train.

---

card When I went to the country, I wrote to my teacher on a **card** called a post card. I put a stamp on the card and mailed it.

Every year we send Christmas **cards.** When my friend has a birthday, I send him a birthday card.

---

care Will your mother **care** if you stay and play? She won't care as long as I come home for dinner.

I **care for** my kittens.

I **look after** my kittens.

I do not **care for** pie.

I do not **like** pie.

---

careful Mary is **careful** when she crosses the street. She watches out for the cars.

---

careless Jane is **careless** when she crosses the street.

Jane is **not careful** when she crosses the street. She doesn't watch out for the cars.

carpenter The man who built our house is a **carpenter.** A carpenter put together the wooden part of our house.

---

carpet We have **carpet** on our living room floor. We have carpet on the stairway. We do not have carpet on the floor of the kitchen.

---

carriage

This is a doll's **carriage.**

Cinderella rode to the party in a carriage.

---

carried I **carried** my dolls to the playhouse in my arms. The truck **carried** the vegetables to market.

---

carrot

A **carrot** is a vegetable. The part of the carrot we eat is the root. We grow **carrots** in the garden. The bunny likes the carrot as much as we do.

---

carry I **carry** the dinner dishes into the kitchen. Our automobile can **carry** five people.

carried I **carried** my dolls to the playhouse in my arms.

carries This hose **carries** water to use in the garden.

cart A **cart** is a **small, light wagon.** A cart may have two wheels or four wheels.

---

case A **case** is a kind of box. We put books in a bookcase. We carry clothes in a suitcase.

In case it rains, we will stay home.

If it rains, we will stay home.

---

castle

A **castle** on a mountain.

---

cat My **cat** is following a bird. "Mew-mew," says the cat. I will not let my cat catch the bird.

---

catch

Jack can **catch** the ball with one hand.

I ran after my big brother and tried to **catch** him.

I ran after my big brother and tried to **get hold of** him.

Take off your wet shoes so that you won't **catch** a cold.

Take off your wet shoes so that you won't **get** a cold.

catches Our dog **catches** rats. Our cat catches mice.

caught Jack **caught** the ball. The dog caught the rabbit.

caterpillar

A **caterpillar** is a **furry kind of worm.** When it grows it becomes a butterfly.

---

cattle These are **cattle** in a pasture.

---

caught Jack **caught** the ball.
Jack **got hold of** the ball.

I **caught** a bad cold when I was out in the snow.
I **got** a bad cold when I was out in the snow.

---

cave

A **cave** is a big hole under the ground. This cave goes into the side of a hill. Many animals live in **caves.**

---

ceiling At the top of our room is the **ceiling.** A fly can walk on the ceiling.

---

cellar The **room under a house** is the **cellar.** A cellar is also called a basement. We have a furnace in our cellar.

cent A **cent** is one **penny.** What can you buy for a cent? Five **cents** is equal to a nickel. Ten cents is equal to a dime.

---

center

The flowers are in the **center** of the table.

The flowers are in the **middle** of the table.

Here is the center of this circle.

---

centimeter This line is one **centimeter** long ——.

---

certain Are you **certain** that you closed the door?

Are you **sure** that you closed the door?

Certain foods are not good for me.

Some foods are not good for me.

---

chain We made a **chain** of colored paper at kindergarten.

---

chair My baby sister has a little rocking **chair.** Daddy has a big chair. They sit in their **chairs.**

chalk We use **chalk** for writing on the blackboard.

---

chance There is a **chance** that snow will fall today.

It may happen that snow will fall today.

Give me a **chance** to hit the ball. It is my turn.

---

change Dora gave the grocer a dollar for some eggs. The eggs cost only sixty cents. The grocer gave Dora the **change.** He gave her the money that was left over from the dollar.

Do you think the weather will **change?**

Do you think the weather will **become different?**

Mother had to **change** Baby's dirty dress. She had to take it off and put on a clean one.

I am going to **change** my dollhouse furniture.

I am going to **move** my dollhouse furniture **around.**

changed I **changed** my shoes because they were wet.

---

chase

The cat will **chase** the mouse.

The cat will **run after** the mouse.

chased I **chased** my big brother around the yard.

---

cheek

Her **cheek** is pink.

The **side of** her **face** is pink.

Both **cheeks** are pink.

cheer We saw Mickey Mouse. We gave a **cheer.**
We gave a **happy shout.**

We are **full of cheer.**
We are **happy.**

When our side wins the game, we **cheer.**
When our side wins the game, we **shout happily.**

---

cheerful We are **cheerful** at Christmas time.
We are **merry and full of good cheer** at Christmas time.

Red is a **cheerful** color.
Red is a **bright** color.

---

cheese **Cheese** is made of milk. There are many kinds of cheese. Do you like cheese?

If all the world were apple pie,
And all the sea were ink,
And all the trees were bread and cheese,
What should we have for drink?

---

cherries Some **cherries** are red. Some are black. Some are yellow. We picked cherries off the cherry tree. Mother made the cherries into a cherry pie.

---

cherry

A **cherry** is a small, round fruit. There was a cherry tree in our yard. Some birds like to eat the **cherries.**

chest

The doctor listens to my heart beat in my **chest.**

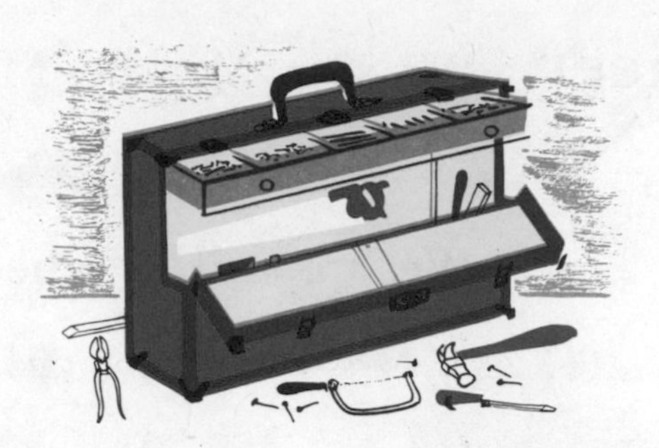

This is a tool **chest.**
This is a tool **box.**

---

chew We **chew** with our teeth. You should chew your food well when you eat. Baby cannot chew yet. She has no teeth.

---

chick

A **chick** is a **baby chicken.** The chick says, "Peep-peep." The **chicks** are running to their mother.

---

chicken A **chicken** is a bird. A mother chicken is a hen and a father chicken is a rooster. The meat of a chicken is good to eat. The **chickens** at Grandmother's farm are white.

---

chief Sitting Bull was a **chief** of the Indians.

Sitting Bull was a **leader** of the Indians. He told them what to do.

child A little boy is a **child.** A little girl is a child, too. I am the child of my father and mother.

---

children Boys and girls are **children.** We have three children in our family.

---

chimney Our house has a big **chimney** to let the smoke of the furnace go out.

Up on the house top, click,
click, click—
Down through the chimney
came good St. Nick.

---

chin

I felt my **chin.**
My chin is under my mouth.
It moves when I talk or eat.

---

chipmunk A **chipmunk** is a small squirrel. It is sometimes called a ground squirrel.

---

chocolate Candy is often made of **chocolate.** We make chocolate from a bean. It is a dark brown color. Do you like chocolate bars? A hot drink can be made of chocolate.

choose You may **choose** one of the roses.

You may **pick out** one of the roses.

chose Jane **chose** the red apple.

chosen I was **chosen** to be the fairy in our play.

---

chop The man will **chop** the tree down with an ax.

The man will **cut** the tree down **by hitting** it with an ax.

This is a lamb **chop.** I like to eat a lamb chop. Don't you?

---

chose Jane **chose** the red apple.

---

chosen I was **chosen** to be a fairy in our play.

Christmas

We receive presents at **Christmas.** We have a Christmas tree, too.

At Christmas play and make good cheer,
For Christmas comes but once a year.

chunk There are **chunks** of meat in the soup.

There are **short, thick pieces** of meat in the soup.

We bought a large chunk of chocolate at the store. Then we broke it into small chunks and ate it.

---

church

This is a **church.** In church people learn about God.

---

churn

The farmer's wife made butter in the **churn.** She beat the cream in the churn, and this made butter.

---

circle

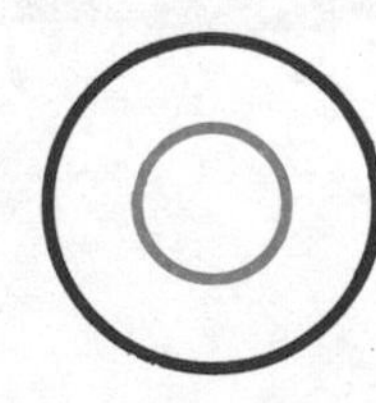

A **circle** is shaped like a ring.

We stand in a circle to play "Drop the Handkerchief."

If you drop a stone in the water it makes **circles.**

circus At the **circus** we saw a giant and a very small man. A clown was riding on the elephant's back. Another clown was feeding a baby pig. There were many clowns. The circus was in a big tent.

We saw the animals do tricks. We saw men and women swinging on high ropes and bars. There were horses, lions, tigers, seals, dogs, elephants and a goat. Can you find all these animals in the picture?

We had fun at the circus. Maybe we will go again next year when the circus comes to town.

city A **city** is a place where many people live close together. My cousins live in the city. I live on a farm in the country. Do you live in the city or in the country?

---

clap  We **clap** for joy.
We **hit our hands together** for joy.

clapped When the play was over, everyone **clapped.**

---

class Barbara belongs to a dancing **class.** There are twelve children in the class. They are learning how to dance.

---

claw  A bird's **claw** is a bird's foot.

The cat scratches with her **claws.** 

---

clay  Ronnie uses **clay** in kindergarten. He makes clay animals and bowls. Clay comes out of the earth. Bricks are made from clay.

clean

Mary's face is **clean.** She washed it. John's face is dirty. He didn't wash it.

Today is Saturday, and I am going to **clean** my room.

cleaned I **cleaned** the spot off my dress.

---

clear It is a **clear** day. The sun is shining, and there are no clouds in the sky.

The water in the lake was so **clear** that we could see the fish. The window glass is clear. You can see through it.

The teacher says, "Children, is that **clear?** Do you understand it?"

---

clever My sister is **clever** at fixing things. She fixed my broken wagon in no time at all.

---

climb

Look at the monkey **climb** the tree.
Look at the monkey **go up** the tree.

climbed Grandfather slowly **climbed** the stairs.

climbing The man was **climbing** the ladder.

cloak A **cloak** is a **loose coat.** Some **cloaks** are made without sleeves.

clock A **clock** tells you what time it is. An alarm clock wakes you up by ringing a bell.

Hickory, dickory, dock,
The mouse ran up the clock,
The clock struck one,
The mouse ran down;
Hickory, dickory, dock.

close I sat **close to** Mother in the auto.

I sat **near** Mother in the auto.

Please **close** the door.

Please **shut** the door.

closed I **closed** the book when I finished reading it.

The book I am reading now is open.

closet I hang my clothes in a **closet.**

I hang my clothes in a **small room.** We have many **closets** in our house.

cloth Our clothes are made of **cloth.** Silk and cotton are two kinds of cloth. Mary is making a doll's dress out of cloth.

---

clothes

Richard is putting on his **clothes.**

Here are Richard's clothes.

---

cloud

Rain comes from a **cloud** in the sky.

See this airplane high up in the **clouds.**

On windy days the clouds move fast.

---

clover The **clover** is a plant that grows on the farm. It grows in our lawn, too. It has a pink or white flower and three leaves. Sometimes you find one with four leaves.

---

clown The **funny man at the circus** was the **clown.** Have you ever acted like a clown?

club

This is a golf **club**.

Mother went to a meeting of her music **club**.

Mother went to a meeting of her music **group**.

---

coach

An old-fashioned carriage was called a **coach.** Now we call a railway car that carries people a coach. Sometimes a bus is called a coach.

The man who teaches the boys to play football and other games is called a **coach.**

---

coarse

The cloth in my coat is **coarse.** It feels rough when you touch it.

---

coast

The **land along the sea or ocean** is called the **coast.** It is also called the seashore.

I am going to **coast** downhill on a sled.

I am going to **slide** downhill on a sled.

coasting

Freddie, Joe, and Bob were **coasting** down the snowy hill on their sleds.

coat

Bob is putting his **coat** on. He is going outdoors.

A bear has a thick **coat** of fur which keeps him warm in winter.

Our house got a **coat** of white paint.

---

cocoa Cocoa is a **hot drink made of chocolate and milk.** I like cocoa.

---

coffee Father and Mother drink **coffee** for breakfast. Coffee comes from the coffee berry.

---

cold I have a **cold.** I sneeze and blow my nose.

Ice cream is **cold.**

Ice cream is **not warm.**

It is cold in winter in the north part of the United States. My hands are cold.

---

collar

John has a red **collar** on his shirt.

Mary has a red collar on her dress.

My dog also has a red collar.

college When I finish high school, I am going to **college.**

When I finish high school, I am going to **a higher school.**

---

color

Red is a bright **color.**

There are four **colors** in my paint box.

I am going to **color** my picture book.

colored I **colored** my picture red and green.

---

colt A **colt** is a **baby horse.**

Here is a colt with his mother.

---

comb  I have my own **comb.**

I use my comb to make my hair smooth.

I comb my hair with it.

I comb my doll's hair, too.

Bees store their honey in a kind of box made of wax. It is called a honeycomb.

A rooster has a red piece on the top of his head. It is called his **comb.**

come Peter wants his puppy to **come** toward him. He says, "Come," but the puppy goes away.

came All the birds **came** to the wedding of Jenny Wren and Cock Robin.

coming When Mother calls me, I say, "I am **coming,** Mother."

---

comic strip A **comic strip** is a **short strip of pictures that tell a story.** Comic strips are also called **comics.** We read comics in the newspaper.

---

company Mother is going to have **company** on her trip. There will be other people with her, so that she won't be alone.

We have **company** at our house.

We have **people visiting** at our house.

The captain leads a **company** of soldiers.

The captain leads a **group** of soldiers.

Daddy works for a big **company.**

---

cook

Mother is a good **cook.**

When you bake or boil food, you **cook** it. When you roast food, you cook it. You cook on a stove.

cooked How are potatoes **cooked?** They are often boiled in a kettle. Sometimes they are baked in the oven.

cooking We work in the kitchen when we are **cooking.**

cookie

Peggy is eating a **cookie.**

---

cool Ice makes water **cool.**

Ice makes water **less warm.**

Mother puts the pies near the window to **cool.** The pies will become less warm.

The day is **cool.**

The day is **not very warm.** We must wear our sweaters.

---

copy I will try to **copy** the picture in the comics.

I will try to **make one just like** the picture in the comics.

---

cord A **cord** is like a **thin rope** or a **thick string.**

---

corn

This is an ear of **corn.** Corn is a grain. The grains of corn grow on ears. Sweet corn is good to eat.

Little Boy Blue, come blow your horn;
The sheep's in the meadow, the cow's in the corn.

corner

Tommy is going to the store on the **corner.**

Daddy left his umbrella in the **corner** of the hall.

Did you ever play "Puss in the Corner?"

---

cost Jack bought a knife. It **cost** him sixty cents. He paid sixty cents for it.

---

cottage A **cottage** is a **small house.**

---

cotton

Here is a **cotton** plant.

Cotton is made into cloth. The cloth is called cotton, too.

Helen's dress is made of cotton.

---

cough I had to **cough** because I had a cold.

could Jane **could** jump the rope.
Jane **was able to** jump the rope.

---

couldn't **Couldn't** is another way to say and write **could not.**
Alice couldn't jump the rope. It was too high.

---

count Can you **count** the roosters in this picture?

One, two, three, four, five. Daddy will count my money for me.

counted He **counted** my pennies. There were ten of them.

---

country

The United States is our **country.**

This is a farm in the **country.** A child who lives on a farm is called a country child.

---

couple Larry has **a couple** of pencils.
Larry has **two** pencils.
Two things of the same kind are a couple.

---

course Can you spell your name? Of **course** I can.
Surely I can.

When a ship changes its **course,** it turns and goes another way.

cousin My uncle and aunt have two children, Jerry and Ellen. Jerry is my **cousin.** Ellen is my cousin, too. The children of all my aunts and uncles are my **cousins.**

---

cover

Frank is taking off the **cover** of the box.

I **cover** my doll with a blanket. I put the blanket over her to keep her warm.

covered We **covered** the seeds with dirt when we planted our garden.

---

cow

Our **cow** gives us milk to drink.

The **cows** eat the grass in the pasture.

The friendly cow all red and white,
I love with all my heart;
She gives me cream with all her might,
To eat with apple tart.

---

cowboy I saw a moving picture with a **cowboy** in it. He rode a horse and drove the cattle. Sometimes I dress like a cowboy.

crack The cup has a **crack** in it, but it is not broken.

We heard a loud **crack** of the gun.
We heard a loud **sound** from the gun.

I like to **crack** nuts.

---

cracker 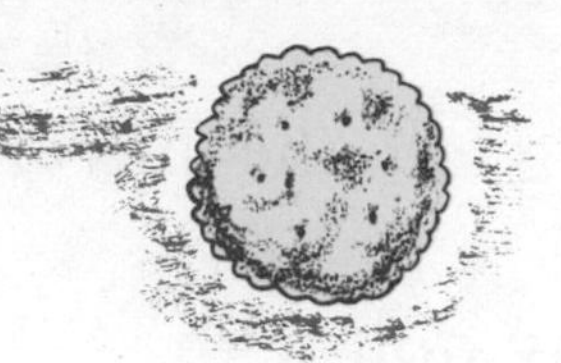 This is a **cracker.**

I like to eat **crackers** with my milk.

---

cradle My baby doll sleeps in a **cradle.**

Rock-a-bye, baby, on the tree-top,
When the wind blows, the cradle will rock;
When the bough breaks, the cradle will fall,
Down will come baby, cradle, and all.

---

crawl See the baby **crawl** on his hands and knees. He cannot walk yet.

---

crayon I am coloring my paper doll with a blue **crayon.**

I am coloring my paper doll with a blue **coloring pencil.** I have eight **crayons** of different colors.

cream The **cream** comes to the top of the milk. Butter is made from cream.

> Curly locks! Curly locks! Wilt thou be mine?
> Thou shalt not wash dishes, nor yet feed the swine,
> But sit on a cushion and sew a fine seam
> And live upon strawberries, sugar, and cream.

---

creep The baby can **creep** on his hands and knees. He cannot walk yet.

I am trying to surprise Daddy. **I creep** behind his chair.
I move slowly and quietly behind his chair.

crept I did not want Bill to hear me. **I crept** quietly through the bushes.

---

cried When Billy hurt his finger, he **cried.** Tears came from his eyes.

---

crooked Don picked up a stick that was **crooked.**
Don picked up a stick that was **not straight.**

The road was very crooked. It had many bends in it.

> There was a crooked man, and he went a crooked mile,
> And he found a crooked six-pence against a crooked stile;
> He bought a crooked cat, which caught a crooked mouse,
> And they all lived together in a little crooked house.

cross

There is a red **cross** on this woman's cap.

I am **cross** today.

I am **angry** today.

We **cross** the river on the bridge.

We **go to the other side of** the river on the bridge.

crossed When the sign said "Go," we **crossed** the street.

---

crow This big black bird is a **crow.** "Caw, caw," says the crow.

The farmer chases the **crows** out of his corn field.

Have you ever heard a rooster **crow?**

He says, "Cock-a-doodle-doo," early in the morning.

crows When the rooster **crows,** he wakes the farmer up.

---

crowd

There is a **crowd** on the beach.

There are **many people** on the beach.

The people **crowd** on to the beach because it is a hot day.

The people **come** on to the beach **in large numbers** because it is a hot day.

The children **crowd** into the bus.

The children **push** into the bus.

crowded We all **crowded** into the little room.

crown

Here is a king with his **crown** on his head. A crown is worn by a king or a queen.

---

crumb A **crumb** fell from my piece of cake.

A **small bit** fell from my piece of cake. In winter we put bread **crumbs** out for the birds.

---

cry Joan will **cry** if she falls down. Tears will come from her eyes.

cried When Bill hurt his finger, he **cried.**

crying When his finger stopped hurting, he stopped **crying.**

---

cup

A **cup** has a handle on it.

Here are two **cups.** One is a cup to drink from. One is a cup to measure with.

---

cupboard

We keep dishes and food in the **cupboard.**

curl I wind my hair around my finger to make a **curl.** Jane has many **curls** in her hair.

I like to **curl** up in a chair and look at a book.

---

curly I wish my hair were **curly** like Jane's.

I wish my hair were **full of curls** like Jane's.

---

curtain

A **cloth hanging over a window or door** is a **curtain.** The **curtains** are blowing at the window.

---

cut

Nancy will **cut** the paper doll.

Bob had a **cut** in his finger.

He **cut** his finger with a piece of glass.

cutting I am **cutting** pictures out of the paper.

---

cute My new kitten is **cute.**

My new kitten is **little and pretty.**

D d

Dad My name for my **father** is **Dad.**

Daddy Mary's name for her **father** is **Daddy.**

daily The newspaper is brought to our house **daily.**
The newspaper is brought to our house **every day.**
The mail comes daily except Sunday.

daisies

These are white **daisies.** There are pink daisies, too.

daisy The **daisy** is a flower that grows in the fields.

dance We **dance** to music.

We **take pretty steps** to music.

danced We **danced** to music on the radio.

dancing Ted and Polly are **dancing** together.

---

dandelion

The **dandelion** is a plant with a yellow flower. This is a dandelion in bloom.

When the dandelion goes to seed, it looks like this.

---

danger A red light often means **danger.** There is danger in crossing the street without looking.

---

dangerous

It is **dangerous** to cross the street when the autos are coming.

It is **not safe** to cross the street when the autos are coming.

---

dare I **dare** you to come off base. I will catch you if you do.

dark At night it is **dark** out of doors.

At night it is **not light** out of doors.

Black is a **dark** color.

---

darling Sometimes Mother calls me her **darling.** She means she loves me very much.

---

dash

I watched Father **dash** water on the fire.

I watched Father **throw** water on the fire. The water put the fire out.

I saw a policeman **dash** after a thief.

I saw a policeman **run quickly** after a thief.

dashed Prince **dashed** around the yard barking loudly.

---

date What **date** is this? The date is March 1. The date on the calendar shows the year, the month, and the day of the month.

A **date** is a fruit. It grows at the very top of a tall tree.

---

daughter A girl is the **daughter** of her mother and father.

day

The **day** is the **time when it is light.**

It is also called the daytime.

The night is the time when it is dark.

The **daytime and the nighttime together** make one **day.** There are twenty-four hours in the day. The first day of the week is Sunday. There are seven **days** in the week.

---

dead

The mouse is **dead.** Something that is dead is **not alive.**

---

dear Robert's father was **dear** to him. Robert loved his father.

Mother says, "Oh **dear!**" when anything is wrong.

December **December** is the **twelfth month of the year.** It has thirty-one days. Christmas comes in December. In some parts of our country it snows in December.

decide Let's **decide** what game we are going to play.

Let's **make up our minds** what game we are going to play.

decided We **decided** to play baseball. I had a cold. Mother decided I was to stay in bed for a day or two.

---

deed Feeding the birds bread crumbs was a good **deed.**

Feeding the birds bread crumbs was a good **thing to do.**

We should do one good deed each day.

---

deep A **deep** hole goes far down in the ground The water in the ocean is deep. It is a long way down before you come to the bottom of the ocean.

---

deer

A **deer** is a wild animal. Some **deer** have horns.

---

deliver The man will **deliver** the package.

The man will **bring and hand to us** the package.

---

den A **den** is a wild animal's home. The squirrel has his den in a hollow tree. The rabbit's den is a hole in the ground.

My big brother calls his room a **den.**

dentist The person that fixes my teeth and cleans them is the **dentist.**

---

desert A **desert** is land without trees or grass. Very little grows in the desert because there is no water there.

---

desk 

Daddy works at his **desk** in the office.

We write and read on a desk.

---

destroy A fire can **destroy** the house by burning it. A storm can destroy the barn by blowing it down.

---

dew In the early morning there is **dew** on the grass in our yard.

In the early morning there are **very small drops of water** on the grass in our yard.

One morning very early, before the sun was up,
I rose and found the shining dew on every buttercup.

---

diamond  A **diamond** is a very pretty stone.

My mother wears a diamond ring.

did Mary **did** her work at school. Lucy did her best to learn the game.

Jim said **I did** not see the parade, but **I** really did.

---

didn't **Didn't** is another word for **did not.** John didn't go to school today.

---

die Flowers **die** when frost comes.

Flowers **do not live any longer** when frost comes.

died The rat **died** when he was caught in the trap.

---

different The colors of these boxes are **different.**

The colors of these boxes are **not alike.**

They have different shapes, too.

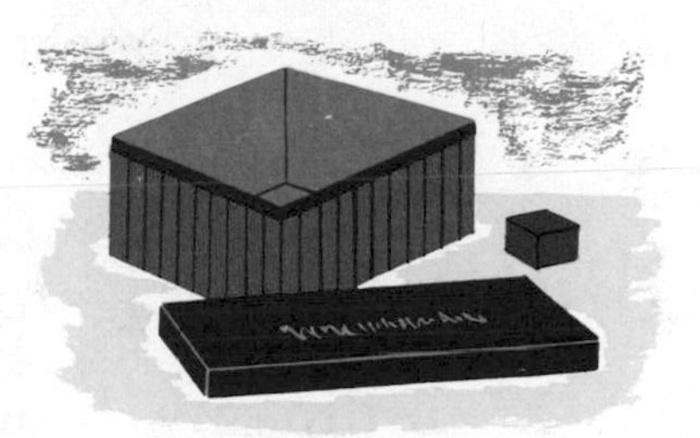

---

dig

Our dog can **dig** a hole to put his bone in.

digging The men are **digging** a big hole in the lot next door. It is for the cellar of the house they will build.

dug We **dug** a hole in our yard and planted a tree there.

dime A **dime** is money. A dime will buy the same as two nickels. It will buy the same as ten cents. Whenever Timothy gets a dime, he puts it in his dime bank.

---

dinner We are eating our **dinner.**

We are eating our **main meal of the day.** We eat dinner in the evening, but some people eat dinner at noon.

---

dinosaur The **dinosaur** was a very large animal that lived many, many years ago. Some dinosaurs were almost 100 feet long.

---

dip I am going to **dip** water out of the lake with my bucket.

I **dip** my hands into the water when I wash them.

---

dirt Sam got **dirt** on his hands. He picked up a piece of coal.

---

dirty

Sam's hands are **dirty.**

Sam's hands are **not clean.**

---

disappear Did you see my dog **disappear** in the tall weeds?

Did you see my dog **go out of sight** in the tall weeds?

disappeared My gloves have **disappeared.** They are lost.

dish

I eat my food from a **dish.**

---

dishes Plates and cups and saucers are **dishes.**

---

ditch I saw a man digging a **ditch** to let the water run in. Water runs in the ditch along the road. A big ditch looks like a small stream.

---

divide When you **divide** a thing, you **make it into parts.** It is not whole any more. Mother will divide the orange between the two of us.

---

do I will **do** all my work today.

Do you like this book? I do.

did Jim said **I did** not see the parade, but I really did.

does The farmer **does** his work every day.

doing What are you **doing?**

done My work is **done.**

My work is **finished.**

doctor

Mary is sick. The **doctor** came to help her get well. A doctor knows how to make you well.

---

does The farmer **does** his work every day.

---

doesn't A short way to say **does not** is **doesn't.** Doesn't that ice cream taste good?

---

dog A **dog** is a tame animal. "Bow-wow," says the dog. The other dog wants to play. Soon the two **dogs** will be friends.

---

doing What are you **doing?**

---

doll

My **doll** is named Judy. She is a rag doll. I have a baby doll, too.

I once had a sweet little doll, dears,
The prettiest doll in the world;
Her cheeks were so red and so white, dears,
And her hair was so charmingly curled.

dollar A **dollar** is money. A dollar will buy as much as one hundred cents. There are paper dollars and silver dollars.

---

done My work is **done.**

My work is **finished.**

---

donkey A **donkey** is an animal with long ears. A donkey looks something like a horse.

Donkey, donkey, old and gray,
Open your mouth and gently bray;
Lift your ears and blow your horn
To wake the world this sleepy morn.

---

don't **Don't** means **do not.** I don't want to go.

---

door Our front **door.**

There are ten **doors** in our house. We have doors to all the rooms, and doors on our cupboards, too.

---

dot A **dot** is a small spot. I made a black dot on white paper. Mary's dress has **dots** in it.

double Our garage has **double** doors. Bee is spelled with a double e.

---

down

When you go **down,** you go **from a higher place to a lower place.**

James is sliding down the slide.

The boys ran down the hill.

---

downstairs Paul is walking **downstairs.**

He was upstairs. I called to him to come downstairs.

---

dozen A **dozen** of anything is **twelve.** I have a dozen colored crayons.

---

drank I **drank** a glass of milk.

---

draw

Peter will **draw** a picture.

drawing Dick uses colored crayons when he is **drawing** a picture.

drew I **drew** a funny picture of Bill.

dream Sally had a **dream** while she was asleep.

Did you **dream** last night?

dreamed I **dreamed** that I was on a picnic.

---

dress My sister wore a pretty **dress** to the party.

I will **dress** in a hurry because I am late.

I will **put on my clothes** in a hurry because I am late.

This is Mary's dancing dress.

This is Mother's dress.

dressed Mother **dressed** the baby in his snowsuit.

---

dresses One of my dolls has three **dresses.**

---

drew I **drew** a funny picture of Bill.

---

drill 

Daddy is making holes in the board with a **drill.**

I **drill** on how to write my name. I write my name again and again.

drink The kitten wants a **drink** of cream.

Susie will **drink** all her cocoa.

drank I **drank** a glass of milk.

drinking  The cow is **drinking** water.

drunk Elsie has **drunk** a quart of milk today.

---

drive Every Sunday we go for a **drive** in our car.

A street is sometimes called a **drive.**

My aunt will **drive** us to school in her car.

Spot can **drive** the chickens out of our garden by barking at them.

driven The dog has **driven** the sheep into the pasture.

drives The farmer **drives** his tractor around his farm.

drove The bus driver **drove** the bus.

---

drive-in A **drive-in** is a place you can drive to and stay in your car while being served. We went to a drive-in and ordered sandwiches.

---

driver A **driver** is a **person who drives.** The driver of the truck is the truck driver. The driver of the airplane is the pilot.

drop

The nurse put a **drop** of medicine in my eye. This is the shape of a **drop.**

The rain falls in **drops.** The drops are like small balls of water.

You can see the rain **drop** from the trees after a storm.

You can see the rain **fall** from the trees after a storm.

I **drop** my book.

I **let** my book **fall.**

dropped Mary **dropped** the cup, but it did not break.

---

drove My mother **drove** our car downtown.

My aunt **drove** us to school in her car.

The dog **drove** the sheep into the pasture.

---

drown If a person is under water and cannot get air to breathe, he may **drown.** Then he will be dead.

---

drum

This is a **drum.**

Bring the comb and play upon it!
Marching, here we come!
Willie cocks his highland bonnet,
Johnnie beats the drum.

---

drunk Elsie has **drunk** a quart of milk today.

dry I will **dry** my doll clothes in the sun.

I will **get the water out of** my doll clothes in the sun.

The sun is shining and the streets are **dry**.

It is dark and rainy and the streets are wet.

drying Billy washed his hair, and now he is **drying it**.

---

duck

A **duck** is a bird that can swim. A duck can walk, too. Wild **ducks** can fly.

Jim will **duck** if I throw the pillow at him.

Jim will **get down and out of the way** if I throw the pillow at him.

---

dug We **dug** a hole in our yard and planted a tree there.

---

during We played **during** recess. We played as long as recess lasted.

---

dust

Alice is sweeping up the **dust.** The wind blows dust in my eyes on a windy day.

We have to **dust** the furniture every day.

E e

each 

The robin will give a worm to **each** little bird.

eagle An **eagle** is a very large bird. Ask your father to let you look at a quarter. There is a picture of an eagle on it.

ear 

A mosquito is biting Larry's **ear.**

You hear with your **ears.**

The rabbit has long ears.

Did you ever eat sweet corn from the **ear?** I like to eat an ear of corn.

early It rained **early** in the morning. It rained before I was awake.

I went to the show **early.** I got there before it started.

---

earn If I mow the lawn, I will **earn** two dollars.

If I mow the lawn, I will **be paid** two dollars **for my work.**

---

earth Harry digs in the **earth.**

Harry digs in the **ground.**

The **earth** is round like a ball. We live on the earth.

---

east

The sun rises in the **east.**

If you look at the sun early in the morning, you will be looking east. East is to your right on a map when you read it.

Easter We color eggs at **Easter.**

We put the eggs in Easter baskets.

---

easy Something that is **easy** to do is **not hard** to do.

It is easy to jump over a crack in the sidewalk. It is not easy to jump over a high fence.

eat

See Jack Sprat and his wife **eat.**

Jack Sprat could eat no fat,
His wife could eat no lean;
And so between the two of them
They licked the platter clean.

ate Kitty **ate** all his food. His plate is empty.

eaten After we had **eaten** dinner, I went to play.

eating I use my spoon and fork when I am **eating.**

---

edge Jerry is looking over the **edge** of a cliff.

A knife has a sharp **edge.**

---

egg

I had an **egg** for breakfast.
Birds lay **eggs** in the nest.
Chickens lay the eggs we eat.

---

eight 8

Five - six	5 - 6
Pick up sticks.	Pick up sticks.
Seven - **eight**	7 - **8**
Lay them straight.	Lay them straight.
Nine - ten	9 - 10
A good fat hen.	A good fat hen.

one	two	three	four	five	six	seven	**eight**	nine	ten	eleven	twelve
1	2	3	4	5	6	7	**8**	9	10	11	12

either I have two kittens. You may have **either** of them. You may have **one or the other of them.**

---

elbow Ralph fell down and got dirt on his **elbow.** His elbow is between the upper and lower parts of his arm. He can bend his arm by using his elbow.

---

electric

An **electric** lamp makes a light to see by. An electric toaster makes heat to toast our bread. An electric iron makes heat to press our clothes.

---

electricity **Electricity** makes the lights go on in stores and houses. Our radios are run by electricity. Machines are often run by electricity.

---

elephant An **elephant** is one of the largest animals.

I asked my mother for fifteen cents
To see the elephant jump the fence;
He jumped so high he touched the sky,
And never came back till the Fourth of July.

eleven II Paul has **eleven** marbles. Paul has 11 marbles.

Ten and one make eleven. 10 + 1 = 11.

one	two	three	four	five	six	seven	eight	nine	ten	**eleven**	twelve
1	2	3	4	5	6	7	8	9	10	11	12

---

elf An **elf** is not a real person, but a kind of fairy. An elf sometimes helps people and sometimes plays tricks on them.

---

else Who **else** is going?

What **other person** is going?

What **else** would you like to eat?

What **other thing** would you like to eat?

Let's go some place **else** now.

Let's go to some **different** place now.

---

empty

One jar is **empty.** It has nothing in it. The other jar is full of cookies.

---

end Our teacher holds the stick by one **end.**

She points the other end at the map.

Let's stay until the **end** of the show.

Let's stay until the **finish** of the show.

enemy An **enemy** is someone who does not like you and may hurt you. Sometimes you fight your **enemy.**

Soldiers fight the **enemy** of their country in war.

---

engine

This **engine** pulls a train. **Engines** make machines go.

The man is fixing the engine in my daddy's car.

An airplane has an engine. I went for a ride in an airplane. We flew through the clouds. The engine made a loud noise.

---

engineer

Here is the **engineer.** He is the man who runs the engine.

---

enjoy When you **enjoy** a thing, you like it and it makes you feel happy. The children enjoy the picnic. I enjoy music.

enjoyed I **enjoyed** seeing the clown do tricks in the circus.

enough I have **enough** money to go to the show.

I have **as much** money **as is needed** to go to the show.

---

enter You **enter** the house through the doorway.

You **go into** the house through the doorway.

---

envelope

Dick put his letter in an **envelope.** He put a stamp on the envelope and gave it to the mailman. The letter in the envelope was written to Dick's mother. He was careful when he wrote the address on the envelope.

---

equal Elizabeth and Jane are of **equal** weight.

Elizabeth and Jane are **the same** weight.

Five cents is **equal** to a nickel. Ten cents is equal to a dime. This sign = means **is equal to.** $2 + 2 = 4$.

---

escape To **escape** means to **get away.** I keep my rabbit in a box so that he won't escape.

Eskimo An **Eskimo** lives in the far north where it is very cold. There is much ice and snow in his land. The Eskimo drives dog teams that pull a sled on the snow.

even

This country is **even.**

This country is not even.
It is hilly.

My puppy is so young that his eyes aren't **even** open.
My puppy is so young that his eyes aren't **yet** open.

Even a baby knows when he is hungry.

The boys were **even** at the end of the race.
The boys were **tied** at the end of the race.

---

evening

The **evening** is the time between sunset and bedtime.

At evening when the lamp is lit,
Around the fire my parents sit;
They sit at home and talk and sing,
And do not play at anything.

---

ever

Have you **ever** seen the cow jump over the moon?
Have you **at any time** seen the cow jump over the moon?

---

every

The farmer gave **every** boy an apple.
The farmer gave **each** boy an apple.

everybody **Everybody** eats.

Every person eats.

Everybody I know likes to eat. Do you?

---

everyone **Everyone** went to the game.

Every person went to the game.

---

everything The children put **everything** in its place.

The children put **each thing** in its place.

---

everywhere Nancy and Terry looked **everywhere** for the ball.

Nancy and Terry looked **every place** for the ball.

On a clear night the stars are **everywhere** in the sky.

On a clear night the stars are **all over** the sky.

---

exact The **exact** price of this doll is one dollar.

The price is not a penny more nor a penny less than a dollar.

---

exactly

This clock says **exactly** 5 o'clock.

This clock says **nearly** 5 o'clock.

except All **except** two children left after school.

All **but** two children left after school.

---

excuse My mother wrote an **excuse** for me to take to my teacher. It said, "Please excuse George. He was ill."

Excuse me, please. I have to go now.

---

expect We **expect** to get a letter today.

We **think we shall** get a letter today.

---

explain I will **explain** how to use the radio. I will explain by telling you.

I will **explain** the puzzle. I will explain by showing you.

---

eye

George is rubbing his **eye.** We have two **eyes.** We see with our eyes.

F f

face 

Emily sees her **face** in the mirror.

When we sit in our class room, we **face** the teacher.

When we sit in our class room, we **turn our faces to** the teacher.

---

fact A **fact** is a **thing that is true.** It is a fact that the world is round. This book tells you many **facts.**

---

factory 

A **factory** is a **building where something is made.** Automobiles are made in a factory. Airplanes are made in a factory.

My father works in a factory where they make books. They have big machines in that factory.

fail Every time I try to catch the ball **I fail.**

Every time I try to catch the ball **I cannot do it.**

Ben will **fail** in school if he does not work harder.

Ben will **not go on to the next grade** in school if he does not work harder. He will **not pass.**

failed Virginia **failed** to jump the high rope.

---

fair Good boys play **fair.**

Good boys play **honestly.**

Isabel has **fair** hair.

Isabel has **light** hair.

We went to the street **fair.**

We went to the street **show.**

fairies Susan, Alice, and I dressed up like **fairies.**

---

fairy

This is a **fairy.** A fairy is not a real person.

Do you like to read **fairy** stories?

---

fall **Fall** is **one of the four seasons of the year.** It is also called autumn.

Watch the snow **fall.**

Watch the snow **come down.**

Baby will **fall** if he tries to walk too fast.

falling The boy is **falling.**

fell

Jack and Jill went up the hill
To fetch a pail of water;
Jack **fell** down and broke his crown,
And Jill came tumbling after.

---

false

This is a **false** face.

This is **not** a **real** face.

Michael told a story that was **false.**

Michael told a story that was **not true.**

---

family I have a mother and father and two brothers. They are my **family.**

fan A **fan** makes a breeze to keep us cool.

This is a paper fan.

This is an electric fan.

I **fan** myself when it is hot.

---

fancy Marilyn's new dress is **fancy.**

Marilyn's new dress is **not plain.** It has much trimming on it.

---

far The hills are **far** away. They are not near.

How **far** is it to your school? Is it a long way or a short way?

My old shoes are **far** too small for me.

My old shoes are **much** too small for me.

---

fare I had to pay **fare** on the bus.

I had to pay **money to ride** on the bus.

---

farm

This is a **farm.** Vegetables, grains, or fruits are grown on a farm. Sometimes there are chickens and cows on a farm.

farmer The **farmer** does the work on a farm.

---

farther I can throw a ball **farther** than Bruce can. I can swim farther than Fred can. Ralph can jump farther than I can.

It is far to Bill's house, but farther to the candy store.

---

fast The wagon goes **fast.**

An auto goes faster than a wagon. An airplane goes faster than an auto. An airplane goes fastest of all.

---

fasten Mary will **fasten** her pocketbook. Then it will stay closed.

---

faster An auto goes **faster** than a wagon.

---

fastest An airplane goes faster than an auto. An airplane goes **fastest** of all.

---

fat

This boy is **fat.**

Bobby Shaftoe's fat and fair,
Combing down his yellow hair,
He's my love for evermair,
Pretty Bobby Shaftoe.

---

father This is my **father.** My father is married to my mother. I call my father "Daddy."

fault It was my **fault** that the dish was broken.

It was my **mistake** that the dish was broken.

---

fear

The rabbits feel **fear** when they see the lion.

They **fear** the lion.

They are **afraid** of the lion.

fears The cat **fears** the dog.

---

feast The Thanksgiving table was spread with a **feast.**

The Thanksgiving table was spread with a **big meal.**

---

feather  Here is a pen made of a **feather.**

This bird is holding a little feather in his bill.

Birds are covered with **feathers.**

February **February** is the **second month in the year.** February has twenty-eight days. Every fourth year it has twenty-nine. Abraham Lincoln's birthday is February 12.

fed The little birds are being **fed.**

The little birds are being **given food.**

---

feed Watch Mother **feed** the baby with a spoon.

Watch Mother **give** the baby **food** with a spoon.

fed The little birds are being **fed.**

feeding We saw them **feeding** the bears at the zoo.

---

feel I **feel** Baby's smooth, soft cheek.

I **touch** Baby's smooth, soft cheek.

I **feel** happy today.

I **am** happy today.

felt I **felt** nice and clean after my bath.

---

feet I have two **feet.** I walk and run on my two feet.

My pony has four feet. I can hop on one foot.

My father is six **feet** tall. A yard is equal to three feet.

fell

Jack and Jill went up the hill
To fetch a pail of water;
Jack **fell** down and broke his crown,
And Jill came tumbling after.

---

fellow He is a jolly good **fellow.**

He is a jolly good **man.**

---

felt I **felt** Baby's smooth, soft cheek.

I **touched** Baby's smooth, soft cheek.

I **felt** nice and clean after my bath.

I **was** nice and clean after my bath.

---

fence

A rail **fence** keeps the cows from running away. A wire fence keeps the chickens from running away.

---

few

Here are a **few** birds.

Here are many birds.

field

Corn grows in a corn **field.** Wheat grows in a wheat field. Both are **fields** of grain.

---

fierce

The **fierce** lion roared.
The **wild** lion roared.

---

fifteen 15

A dime and a nickel make **fifteen** cents.
A dime and a nickel make **15** cents.

ten	**fifteen**	twenty	twenty-five	thirty
10	**15**	20	25	30

---

fifth

Thursday is the **fifth** day of the week. There are four days before Thursday.

first	second	third	fourth	**fifth**
1st	2nd	3rd	4th	**5th**

---

fifty 50

Half a dollar is **fifty** cents.
Half a dollar is **50** cents.

ten	twenty	thirty	forty	**fifty**	sixty
10	20	30	40	**50**	60

fight 

See the lion and the tiger **fight.** They scratch and bite each other.

---

figure This is the **figure** 3.

This is the **number** 3. Numbers are often called figures.

My toy airplane has the **figure** of an aviator in the seat. My toy airplane has the **shape** of an aviator in the seat.

---

fill 

I will **fill** the basket with cherries. Then it will hold no more. It will be full.

filled Father **filled** the auto tank with gasoline.

filling John is **filling** the pail with water.

---

film A **film** is a **thin coating** or a **thin sheet.** There is a film of ice on the pond. We put a roll of film in the camera to take pictures. A film is also a movie.

---

finally My dog had been gone two days. He **finally** came home. He **at last** came home.

find

Let us **find** kitty.
Let us **look for and get** kitty.

found I **found** my kitty. She was hiding under a bush.

---

fine It is a **fine** day.
It is a **sunny, bright** day.

You're looking **fine.**
You're looking **well.**

A spider's web is made of **fine** threads.
A spider's web is made of **small** threads.

Daddy will have to pay **a fine** for parking in the wrong place.
Daddy will have to pay **money** for parking in the wrong place.

---

finger

I have one **finger** up on one hand, and five **fingers** up on the other hand. I pick things up with my fingers.

---

fingernail I have a **fingernail** on the end of each finger. I keep my **fingernails** clean.

---

finish We will **finish** our work very soon.
We will **come to the end of** our work very soon.

finished Mother **finished** my dress. I can wear it now.

fire A **fire** does good things. A fire makes us warm. It burns with a beautiful, bright light. It cooks food. A fire does bad things, too. It can destroy houses and buildings if people are not careful with it. It will burn your skin if you touch it.

---

fireman The **fireman** is holding the hose. He is helping to put the fire out.

---

fire truck See the **fire truck.** It carries hose to throw water on the fire.

---

fireplace A fire is burning in the **fireplace.**

---

first Robert is the **first** boy in line. There is no one in front of him.

One is the first number. There are no numbers before one.

first	second	third	fourth	fifth
1st	2nd	3rd	4th	5th

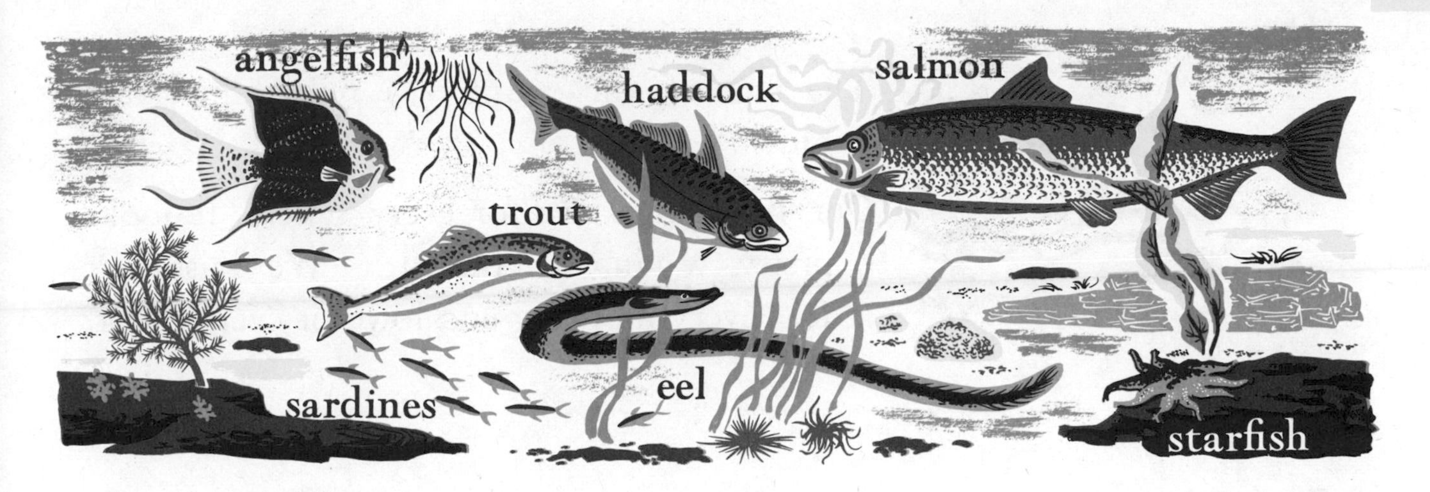

fish A **fish** lives in the water. We had fish for dinner. It was good.
Daddy likes to **fish.**
Daddy likes to **catch fish.**

---

fit George wants his hat to **fit** his head.
George wants his hat to **be the right size** for his head.
Mary has grown so big that her dress won't fit her.

---

five 5

One, two, three, four, **five,**
I caught a hare alive;
Six, seven, eight, nine, ten,
I let her go again.

1, 2, 3, 4, 5,
I caught a hare alive;
6, 7, 8, 9, 10,
I let her go again.

one	two	three	four	**five**	six	seven	eight	nine	ten	eleven	twelve
1	2	3	4	5	6	7	8	9	10	11	12

---

fix I broke my toy. Daddy will **fix** it.
Daddy will **put** it **together again.**
Daddy will **make** it **work right again.**

flag

The **flag** of our country is red, white, and blue.

Our flag has a star for every state. It looks pretty waving in the air. We raise our flag every morning and lower it every night.

---

flame The light you see when a fire burns is the **flame.** The flames are red and yellow.

---

flat The top of a table is **flat.**

The top of a table is **straight and even.** Daddy is making the board flat.

Sam lay **flat** on his back to look at the clouds.

Sam lay **spread out** on his back to look at the clouds.

---

flew

The birds **flew** over the water.

The birds **went through the air** over the water.

float Wood will **float** on water, but a rock will sink.

Wood will **stay on the top** of water, but a rock will sink.

Bill is sitting on a log that **floats** on the water.

---

flock A **group of animals of one kind** is sometimes called a **flock.**

A flock of chickens.

A flock of sheep.

---

floor I have a rag rug on the **floor** of my bedroom. We do not have rugs on our kitchen floor.

Our attic is the third **floor** of our house.

---

flour Wheat is ground into **flour.** Mother makes cake and bread with flour.

flower

A rose is one kind of **flower**.

Other **flowers** are pansies, violets, and lilies.

Roses red and violets blue,
And all the sweetest flowers, that in the forest grew.

---

flown The wild ducks have **flown** south for the winter.

---

fly

The **fly** is on the sugar bowl.

Birds **fly** with their wings.

Birds **go through the air** with their wings.

The pilot will **fly** his plane.

flew The birds **flew** over the water.

flown The wild ducks have **flown** south for the winter.

flying The airplane is **flying** very fast.

---

fold

Helen can **fold** the towels and sheets.

follow Jane's little brother will **follow** her.

Jane's little brother will **come after** her. The children are playing "Follow the Leader."

followed The calf **followed** its mother into the barn.

---

food We eat **food.** Meat is a food. Fruits and vegetables are food. Milk is a food. We have food to eat at breakfast, lunch and dinner. We give food to our dog in his dish. The horse eats grass for his food.

---

fool I was a **fool.** I did not use good sense.

Daddy was trying to **fool** Baby. He was pretending to be a bear.

---

foot Ben kicks the football with his right **foot.** He wears heavy football shoes on his feet.

1 **foot** = 12 inches.

---

football  The man is going to throw the **football.**

There are eleven players on a **football** team.

We go to see football games when our school team plays. We cheer for our side.

for We used a sheet **for** a curtain at our show.

We used a sheet **in place of** a curtain at our show.

Mother came **for** me.

Susan is dressed **for** a party.

I asked **for** a bicycle **for** my birthday.

When I grow up, I'm going to work **for** my father.

How much did you pay **for** your candy?

---

forest 

A **forest** is a **large wood of many trees.** We walked on a path that went through the forest. There were many birds and wild animals in the forest.

---

forget I hope that I do not **forget** my books. I will try to remember to take them with me.

Did you **forget** your new teacher's name? You must try to keep it in mind.

forgot Mary **forgot** her doll.

forgotten I have **forgotten** where I left my cap.

---

fork 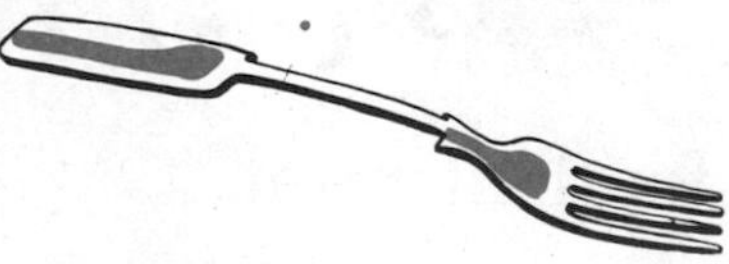

We eat with a **fork.**

We use a knife to cut our food, and a fork to lift it to our mouths.

forty 40 Four dimes equal **forty** cents.

Four dimes equal **40** cents.

ten	twenty	thirty	**forty**	fifty	sixty
10	20	30	**40**	50	60

---

forward Walk **forward.**

Walk **ahead.** You can walk backward, but it is easier to walk forward.

---

fought The lion and the tiger **fought.** They scratched and bit each other.

The soldiers **fought** bravely.

---

found I **found** my kitty.

I looked for and got my kitty. She was hiding under a bush.

---

fountain Water comes out of a **fountain.**

The children are playing around the fountain.

This is a drinking fountain.

four 4

One — two	1 — 2
Buckle my shoe.	Buckle my shoe.
Three — **four**	3 — **4**
Shut the door.	Shut the door.
Five — six	5 — 6
Pick up sticks.	Pick up sticks.

one	two	three	**four**	five	six	seven	eight	nine	ten	eleven	twelve
1	2	3	**4**	5	6	7	8	9	10	11	12

---

fourth April is the **fourth** month of the year. There are three months before April.

first	second	third	**fourth**	fifth
1st	2nd	3rd	**4th**	5th

Fourth of July On the **Fourth of July**, 1776, the people of our country decided to be free. The Fourth of July is also called Independence Day.

---

fox

A **fox** is a wild animal with beautiful fur. Here is a red fox.

---

foxes Some **foxes** are gray. Foxes look like dogs.

free The water in the drinking fountain is **free.**

The water in the drinking fountain **costs nothing.**

The people in our country are **free.**

---

freeze Cold makes water **freeze.**

Cold makes water **change to ice.** The lake will freeze on top when winter comes.

When you make ice cream, you must **freeze** it.

Mother said, "If you go out to play in this cold weather, you'll **freeze.**"

Do you think **it will freeze** tonight?

Do you think **frost will come** tonight?

froze It was so cold that I almost **froze.**

frozen We cannot skate on the river until it has **frozen** hard.

---

freight The **freight** is the **load the freight train carries.** This freight train is carrying oil, machinery, and coal. The oil, machinery, and coal are the freight.

fresh The vegetables are **fresh.** We just picked them out of the garden.

I will get a **fresh** piece of paper, one that has never been used.

When we open the window, **fresh** air comes in. It is clean and cool.

Friday **Friday** is the **sixth day of the week.** Friday is the last day of the school week.

Sunday Monday Tuesday Wednesday Thursday **Friday** Saturday

---

friend Grace is my **friend.** I like her and do things for her. We like to be together.

---

frog

The **frog** is sitting at the edge of the water.

The frog by nature is both damp and cold,
Her mouth is large, her belly much will hold.

---

from Betty is tired **from** jumping rope.

I took a penny **from** my pocket.

Our house is a long way **from** the school.

We got a letter **from** my aunt today.

front

This is the **front** of our house. The front of our house is the part nearest the street.

Daddy is standing **in front of** the fireplace.

Daddy is standing **before** the fireplace.

---

frost The **frost** is **frozen dew.**

It was a cold morning. There was frost on my window. We drew pictures in the frost. Everything outdoors was covered with a white frost.

---

froze It was so cold that the water **froze.**

It was so cold that the water **changed to ice.**

It froze last night and killed the flowers.

Frost came last night and killed the flowers.

My mother **froze** the ice cream in the freezer. Ice cream made at home has a good taste. We like to eat it.

---

frozen We cannot skate on the river until it has **frozen** hard.

---

fruit An orange is a **fruit.** Apples, peaches, and grapes are **fruit,** too. Here is a bowl full of different kinds of fruit.

full When a bucket is **full** of water, it cannot hold any more water.

When anything is full, it cannot hold any more.

---

fun The children are skating. They are having **fun.**

The children are skating. They are having **a good time.**

---

funnel A **funnel** is a tube that is wide at one end and narrow at the other.

---

funny • Donald Duck is **funny.** He makes us laugh.

---

fur

These animals have lots of **fur** on them. My mother has a coat made of fur.

---

furnace We heat our house with a **furnace.**

We heat our house with a **big stove.** We burn gas in our furnace.

Our furnace is in the basement of the house.

---

furniture The chairs, tables, and beds in our house are **furniture.**

Daddy made me some furniture for my doll house.

G g

gallon There are four quarts in a **gallon.** We took a gallon bottle of lemonade to the picnic. Daddy had ten **gallons** of gasoline put into the car before we left.

gallop Have you seen a horse **gallop?**

Have you seen a horse **run as fast as he can?**

game We play a **game** to have fun. We learned two new **games** today. They were baseball and basketball.

garage We keep our car in the **garage.**

garden 

Our **garden** has flowers and vegetables in it.

Mistress Mary, quite contrary,
How does your garden grow?
With cockle shells, and silver bells,
And pretty maids all in a row.

gas The stove in our kitchen burns **gas.** Our meals are cooked on a gas stove. Some people have electric stoves.

Gas is a short word for **gasoline.**

---

gasoline We buy **gasoline** for our car at the filling station. The gasoline makes our automobile go. Gasoline makes the airplane go, too.

---

gate

The boy is leading the cows through the **gate.**

We have a gate on our stairs to keep the baby from falling down.

The gate in front of our house is painted white. We keep it closed.

---

gather Mother will **gather** the children and take them home.

Mother will **get** the children **together** and take them home.

---

gave Bill **gave** me an orange. He did not ask me to pay for it.

---

gaze Rosita likes to **gaze** at the animals in the zoo.

Rosita likes to **look** at the animals in the zoo.

geese

These are **geese.** One is called a goose.

---

general There is a **general** in an army. A general is the head man in an army.

---

gentle My sister is very **gentle.**

My sister is very **kind and nice.**

My mother gave me a **gentle** pat.

My mother gave me a **soft, light** pat.

---

gently

I handle my cat **gently.**

I handle my cat **in a gentle way.**

---

get Polly will **get** the book for you.

I will **get** to school on time.

If you play hard, you **get** tired.

Will you **get** a present for your birthday?

I get up early every morning but Saturday.

getting Bobby has been **getting** good grades in school.

got **I got** a cold because **I got** my feet wet.

giant

A **giant** is a very big and very strong man in a fairy story.

When a real man is very big and very strong, he is sometimes called a **giant.**

---

gift

A **gift** is something that is given to you or something that you give to someone. A gift is also called a present. I have a Christmas gift for Mother. I got many birthday **gifts** from my friends.

---

gingerbread

We like to eat **gingerbread** with our milk.

We like to eat **cake made with ginger** with our milk.

Mother made me a gingerbread man.

---

giraffe

The **giraffe** is an animal with long legs and a very long neck. His neck is so long that he can eat leaves from the tree branches.

---

girl

Peggy is a **girl.** A girl grows up to be a woman. These **girls** are playing house. Peggy will serve tea to her girl friends.

give My playmate will **give** me one of his marbles. I will not have to pay for it.

gave Bill **gave** me an orange.

given I was **given** a puppy for my birthday.

giving I am **giving** Mother a present of a pretty rose.

---

glad Mary is **glad** to go skating.
Mary is **happy** to go skating.

---

glass We drink water from a **glass.**

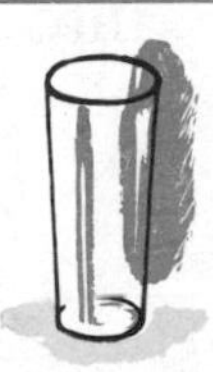

We can see through the window because it is **glass.**

---

glasses These are my **glasses** to help me see better.

---

glove

The **glove** is yellow. The mitten is red. Mother wears **gloves** on her hands. I wear warm gloves or mittens in winter.

---

glue We use **glue** to stick things together.
I will **glue** the leg back on to my doll's chair.

go The sign says, "Go." The automobiles can **go.**

The automobiles can **move forward.**

You must wind the clock, or it won't **go.**

You must wind the clock, or it won't **run.**

Every morning I **go** to school, and every afternoon I come home.

Where does that path **go?** It goes to the swimming pool.

How do the words of that song **go?** I can't remember them.

All Don's toys **go** into that big box.

All Don's toys **belong** in that big box. They are kept there.

goes The boy **goes** up the hill on his bicycle.

going I am **going** to the party.

I am **going** to have fun when I get there.

gone We tried to catch the rabbit, but he was **gone.**

We tried to catch the rabbit, but he was **not there.**

went Joe **went** to his grandfather's farm yesterday.

---

goat

A **goat** is an animal.

Goats have horns. Sam has a goat that pulls his wagon. Sam drives the goat and wagon all around the farm. He feeds his goat hay and oats and gives him water.

gobble Our turkey says, "**Gobble,** gobble."

Mother says, "Don't **gobble** your food."

Mother says, "Don't **eat** your food **too fast.**"

God **God's** in His heaven:
All's right with the world.

---

goes The boy **goes** very fast on his bicycle.

The boy **moves forward** very fast on his bicycle.

An electric clock **goes** without winding.

An electric clock **runs** without winding.

Daddy **goes** to work in the morning and comes home at night.

Do you know where that path **goes?**

That song **goes** like this.

My bicycle **goes** in the garage.

---

going I am **going** to the party. I am **going** to have fun when I get there.

---

gold

Gold is a shiny, yellow metal.

Bobby has a **gold** watch. He can see what time it is when he looks at his watch. Bobby got the gold watch for a birthday present.

goldfish

See the **goldfish** swimming.

---

golf My parents like to play **golf**. It is a game played with a ball and clubs.

---

gone We tried to catch the rabbit, but he was **gone.**

We tried to catch the rabbit, but he was **not there.**

Do you know the fastest an airplane has ever **gone?**

Do you know the fastest an airplane has ever **moved forward?**

---

good Jane is a **good** girl. She does her school work. She helps her parents. She helps others have fun.

---

goodbye

The children waved **goodbye.**

The coach is at the door at last;
The eager children mounting fast
And kissing hands in chorus sing:
Goodbye, goodbye to everything.

---

good morning When I get up, Mother says, "**Good morning,** Nancy."

good night When I go to bed at night, Mother says, "**Good night**, Nancy."

---

goose The **goose** is a bird that looks something like a duck. The red goose is swimming in the pond. The other **geese** have just come out.

Goosey, goosey, gander,
Whither shall I wander?
Upstairs and downstairs
And in my lady's chamber.

---

got I **got** the book for my teacher.

I hurried and **got** to school on time.

I **got** a cold because I **got** my feet wet.

George **got** a sled for his birthday.

Sally **got** up late this morning.

---

grab Ruth tried to **grab** the toy Andy was playing with.

Ruth tried to **take suddenly** the toy Andy was playing with.

---

grade I am in the second **grade** in school.

I am in the second **year** in school.

I got a good **grade** on my test. My grade was 100.

grain The farmer grows **grain.** Wheat, oats, and rye are **grains.**

rye

wheat

oats

One seed of wheat, oats, or rye is called a **grain.** See the tiny **grains** in the farmer's hand.

---

grand Our library is a **grand** building.

Our library is a **large and beautiful** building.

---

grandfather Your **father's father** is your **grandfather.** Your **mother's father** is your **grandfather,** too.

---

grandma **Grandma** is a pet name for **grandmother.**

---

grandmother Your **father's mother** is your **grandmother.** Your **mother's mother** is your **grandmother,** too.

---

grandpa **Grandpa** is a pet name for **grandfather.**

---

grape

A **grape** is a small round fruit that grows in bunches.

Mother puts a bunch of **grapes** into the dish.

grapefruit A **grapefruit** is a fruit. It is round and yellow, and larger than an orange. **Grapefruit** grow on trees.

---

grass Green **grass** grows in our yard. Father cuts the grass when it grows too high. Sometimes I help cut the grass.

---

grasshopper

A **grasshopper** is a bug.

Grasshoppers can jump high.

---

gray

Gray is a color.

Joan's new coat and hat are gray.

---

great George Washington was the first **great** president of our country.

Look at that **great** elephant!

Look at that **very big** elephant!

---

green green This is the color **green.** The leaves of this plant are **green.** We mix blue and yellow paint to make **green** paint.

grew

The little colt **grew** until he was a swift, beautiful horse.

The little colt **got larger** until he was a swift, beautiful horse.

---

grocery

My mother buys our food at the **grocery.**

---

ground

Jerry dug a hole in the **ground.**

Jerry dug a hole in the **earth.**

The butcher **ground** the meat.

The butcher **cut up** the meat **into small pieces.**

---

group A **group** is **several people together.** A group of boys were playing marbles.

A **group** is **several things together.** We saw a group of oak trees in the park.

grow Plants, animals, and people **grow.**

Plants, animals, and people **get larger.** A little plant can grow to be a big plant. A kitten can grow to be a cat. A boy can grow to be a man.

grew The little colt **grew** until he was a swift, beautiful horse.

growing It is spring. All the trees and plants are **growing.**

grows Judy **grows** fast because she eats food that is good for her.

---

growl Does your dog ever **growl?** When a dog growls, he says, "G-r-r-r."

My dog doesn't growl, but he barks.

---

grows Judy **grows** fast because she eats food that is good for her.

Judy **gets larger** fast because she eats food that is good for her.

---

guard

The soldier will **guard** the gate. He will watch to see that no one goes in.

The United States Coast **Guard** protects the shores of our country.

---

guess I said the stone was in Larry's left hand. I made a good **guess.**

I was right. Bill's **guess** was wrong.

Mary must **guess** the answer to the riddle.

Mary must **try to think of** the answer to the riddle.

guest We had a **guest** at home.

We had **someone visiting** at home.

---

guide A **guide** is a **person who shows people the way.**

Will you **guide** me through the woods?

Will you **show** me **the way** through the woods?

---

gum Chewing **gum** is made in thin, flat sticks. We chew gum, but we do not swallow it. Chewing gum tastes good.

---

gun

We shoot with a **gun.**

The cowboy has a gun.

There are many kinds of **guns.**

A	B	C	D	E
F	G	H	I	J
K	L	M	N	O
P	Q	R	S	T
U	V	W	X	Y
		Z		

H h

ha When I laugh, I say, "**Ha,** ha!"

---

had Elizabeth **had** a toy.

Elizabeth **owned** a toy.

I **had** my doll in my arms.

I **held** my doll in my arms.

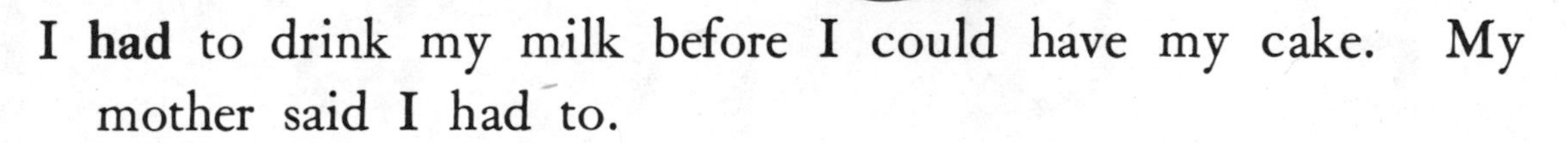

I **had** to drink my milk before I could have my cake. My mother said I had to.

We **had** a good time at the picnic yesterday.

Mother called me, but I **had** started home already.

---

hair 

My mother's **hair** is beautiful.

half

John cut the apple **in half.**

John cut the apple **in two parts, each the same size.** He kept one half. He gave Nancy the other half.

---

hall The rooms of our house open from the **hall.**

We have a very big room at school. It is a **hall.**

Halloween

Halloween is the last night in October. On Halloween we dress up and wear false faces.

---

hammer

I can drive nails with a **hammer.**

---

hand

I have five fingers on each **hand.** Here I hold up my **hands** to show Mother that they are clean. I pick up things with my hands. I hold things with my hands. I use my hands when I work and when I play.

A clock has **hands** to point at the hour and the minute.

Will you please **hand** me that book.

Will you please **give** me that book **with your hand.**

handkerchief I carry a **handkerchief** in my pocket. I blow my nose in my handkerchief.

---

handle

We hold a pitcher by its **handle.**

A cup has a handle. A spade has a handle, too.

Susan must **handle** her puppy gently. Susan handles her puppy with her hands. When she picks the puppy up, or holds him, or gives him a bath, she is handling him.

---

hang

Let us **hang** the birdhouse on the branch of the tree.

hanging We laughed at the monkey **hanging** by its tail.

hangs The coat **hangs** on the hook.

hung The picture was **hung** on the wall by its wire. The monkey hung from the tree by its tail.

---

hangar

A **hangar** is a **building to keep airplanes in.**

hangs The coat **hangs** on the hook.

---

happen When did the accident **happen?**
Something nice will happen tonight.

happened The fire **happened** when I was near the house.

---

happy Peggy is smiling. She is **happy.**

The three little kittens are happy because they have found their mittens.

---

hard The rock is **hard.** The pillow is soft.

Henry jumped over the big snowball.

That was a **hard** thing to do.

That was **not** an **easy** thing to do.

---

hardly We **hardly** had time to eat our dinner.

We **only just** had time to eat our dinner.

I could hardly breathe after running so hard.

---

harm

Sally will not **harm** the butterfly.
Sally will not **hurt** the butterfly.

has Mary **has** a big doll.

Mary **owns** a big doll.

She **has** the doll in her arms.

She **holds** the doll in her arms.

She **has to** take good care of it.

She **must** take good care of it.

Jane always **has** fun when she plays with Mary.

Jane **has** played until she is tired.

---

hat

I show Daddy my new **hat.**

Daddy is wearing a new hat, too. We like our new **hats.**

My hat is made of straw. Mother bought it for me.

---

hatch The hen will **hatch** the eggs by sitting on them.

When a chick hatches out of the shell, it looks like this.

---

hate I **hate** snakes. I like dogs.

hates A lion fears and **hates** an elephant.

have The children **have** a pig, a pony, and a rabbit.

The children **own** a pig, a pony, and a rabbit.

I **have** a penny in my hand.

I **hold** a penny in my hand.

We **have to** go to school at eight o'clock.

We **must** go to school at eight o'clock.

I know I will **have** a good time at the picnic.

I **have** thought of a name for my new puppy.

had I **had** a toy. I lost it. I had a blue dress. It is worn out now.

has Mary **has** a big doll.

---

haven't **Haven't** is another way to say and write **have not.** I haven't a penny.

---

hay

The farmer cuts long grass to make **hay.**

When the grass has dried in the sun, it will be hay. Then the farmer stores the hay in his barn. Horses and cows eat hay. We like to play in the hay.

---

he My father is shaving. **He** is shaving with his razor. He has to shave every day.

head The **head** is the top part of the body. Your eyes, nose, and mouth are in your head.

You could just see the **heads** of the children over the top of the wall.

John is at the **head** of the line. He is first in line.

"You are old, Father William," the young man said,
"And your hair has become very white;
And yet you incessantly stand on your head—
Do you think, at your age, it is right?"

---

health Joan has good **health.** She is not sick.

When there is nothing wrong with your body, you are in good health.

When there is something wrong with your body, you are in bad health.

---

healthy Harry is **healthy.**

Harry is **not sick.**

---

hear I **hear** with my ears. I hear the thunder. I hear the music. I hear my mother reading me a story.

Mother says to Mrs. Young, "What do you **hear** from your boy in the army?" She means, "What does he write in his letters?"

heard I **heard** Bill calling me. I heard my dog barking in the yard.

heart My valentine is shaped like a **heart.**

Can you feel your **heart** beat?

---

heat **Heat** makes you feel warm. You can feel the heat from the sun.

You can feel the heat coming from the furnace.

Mother will **heat** the water on the stove.

Mother will **make** the water **hot** on the stove.

---

heavy

A piano is **heavy.**

A piano is **hard to lift.**

A feather is not heavy.

My breath will lift it.

I must be careful when I lift heavy things.

---

heel

My **heel** is the back part of my foot. I have two **heels.**

I have **heels** on my shoes. My socks have heels, too. I have a hole in the heel of my sock.

---

held Polly **held** a candle in her hand. John held on to the rope.

hello We say **hello** when we meet someone we know. I say, "Hello, Jack." Jack says, "Hello, Mary."

---

help Brother will **help** Baby to walk by holding her hand.

My teacher will **help** me with my school work by explaining it.

I cannot **help** sneezing when I have a cold. I sneeze whether I want to or not.

helped I **helped** Mother think of a Christmas gift for Father.

helping Jerry is **helping** Joan on to the horse.

---

hen

The **hen** is sitting on the nest. The rooster is standing near her. A hen and a rooster are chickens.

Hickety pickety, my black hen,
She lays eggs for gentlemen;
Sometimes nine and sometimes ten,
Hickety pickety, my black hen.

---

her Lucy is my friend, so I let **her** play with my doll.

She let me play with **her** doll.

---

here Why didn't I see my book? It's right **here.**

It's right **in this place.**

hers The dress belongs to Mary. The dress is **hers.**

---

herself Jill hurt **herself** when she was jumping rope.

Mrs. Smith **herself** said so.

The new girl was standing **by herself.**

The new girl was standing **alone.**

---

hid Peter Rabbit **hid** in the grass. He was out of sight.

---

hidden Our Easter eggs were **hidden** in the dining room. We had to hunt for them.

---

hide I will **hide** in the bushes so that no one can see me.

hid Peter Rabbit **hid** in the grass. He was out of sight.

hidden Our Easter eggs were **hidden** in the dining room. We had to hunt for them.

---

high The top of the mountain is **high.** It is far above the valley.

The hook is too **high** for Bobby to reach. It is too far above his head.

higher The yellow dish is high in the cupboard. The white dish is **higher.**

highest The black dish is the **highest** of all.

hill

There is a **hill** near our house. Far away there are mountains. Mountains are much bigger than **hills.**

There was an old woman
Lived under a hill,
And if she's not gone,
She lives there still.

him I gave my toy gun to the boy. I wanted **him** to have it. Now it belongs to him.

himself George rolls **himself** up in the blanket when he sleeps outdoors.

The boy **himself** took the book.

Ben was walking down the street **by himself.**

Ben was walking down the street **alone.**

his The bicycle belongs to Fred. The bicycle is **his.**

His bicycle is painted red.

hit 

Tom will **hit** the ball with his tennis racket.

The carpenter hit the nail with the hammer.

I fell down and hit my knee on the sidewalk.

---

hive A **hive** is a **little house that bees live in.** The bees fly in and out of their hive.

---

hoe I cut the weeds with my **hoe.** I dig in the garden with my hoe.

I dig a hole in the sand with my hoe.

---

hog When a pig grows, he becomes a **hog.**

---

hold Ruth will **hold** the ball in her hand. Robert can hold on to the rope.

held Polly **held** a candle.

---

hole 

The owl lives in a **hole** in the tree.

Daddy made a hole in the wall for the stove pipe.

hollow

Sometimes an old tree trunk is **hollow.**

A rubber ball is often hollow. A balloon is hollow. It has nothing in it but air.

---

home Jim is going **home.**

Jim is going to **the place where he lives.**

---

honest My daddy is an **honest** man. He will not lie or steal.

---

honey Bees make **honey.** Here is honey in the comb. Here is a jar of honey taken from the comb. The honey is sweet.

The King was in the counting-house
Counting out his money;
The Queen was in the parlor
Eating bread and honey.

---

honk The driver will **honk** at the boy on the bicycle.

The driver will **blow his horn** at the boy on the bicycle.

---

hood My raincoat has a **hood.**

My raincoat has a **covering that goes over my head.**

hook

This is a **hook** to
hang your coat on.

This is a fish **hook.**

We catch fish with a fish hook.

---

hop

See the rabbit **hop!**
See the rabbit **jump!**

I can **hop** on one foot.

---

hope

I **hope** to go with Mother.
I **wish** to go with Mother.

---

horn

Jimmy got a **horn** for Christmas. He is blowing his horn. It makes a loud noise.

Some people in a band play **horns.**

Some animals have **horns**
on their heads.

horse The **horse** is an animal. Two horses pulling together are called a team of **horses**.

hose  We use a garden **hose** to water the garden. Firemen use a bigger hose to put water on a fire.

Stockings are often called **hose.**

---

hospital People go to the **hospital** when they are sick. They go to the hospital to get well.

---

hot The bowl of soup is **hot.** The fire is hot. The sun is hot. I get hot when I go out in the sun.

---

hotel A **hotel** is a place to live when you are away from home. You can eat and sleep in a hotel. People pay money to live in a hotel.

---

hour An **hour** is a measure of time. There are sixty minutes in an hour. There are twenty-four **hours** in a day. You can tell what hour it is by the clock.

---

house  A **house** is a building where people live. Here are many **houses.** My house is made of red brick. Mary lives in a house built of wood. Tom's house is across the street. It is painted gray.

how The doctor says: "**How** are you? Do you feel good?"

Next he says: "**How** old are you? How tall are you? How much do you weigh?"

Then he shows me **how** to stick out my tongue so that he can look at it.

Then he shows me **the way** to stick out my tongue so that he can look at it.

---

hug 

Mamma says, "Give me a **hug,** dear."

I hug Mamma. **I** put my arms around Mamma and hold her tight.

---

hundred A dollar equals a **hundred** cents.

A dollar equals **100** cents.

---

hung The picture was **hung** on the wall by its wire.

The monkey hung from the tree by its tail.

---

hungry The dog was **hungry.**

The dog **wanted food.** When I get home from school, I am hungry.

hunt

My dad likes to **hunt.**

I must **hunt for** my teddy bear.

I must **look for and try to find** my teddy bear.

If I hunt everywhere for my teddy bear I will find him.

hunted We **hunted** everywhere for the lost book.

hunting The boys and father went **hunting.**

Bye, baby bunting,
Daddy's gone a-hunting,
To get a little rabbit's skin
To wrap the baby bunting in.

---

hurrah Bob yelled, "**Hurrah,** we won!"

---

hurry My mother can **hurry.**

My mother can **walk fast.**

I must **hurry** and get dressed.

I must **move fast** and get dressed.

If I hurry I will be on time for the party. If I do not hurry I will be late. Whenever we go any place I hurry to get ready.

hurt

Tommy **hurt** his thumb. He hit it with the hammer.

My shoes hurt my feet. They are too tight.

Mother says, "I guess it won't **hurt** you to go without your rubbers."

Mother says, "I guess it won't **be bad for** you to go without your rubbers."

---

husband A **husband** is the **man a woman is married to.** My father is my mother's husband. My father and mother are husband and wife.

---

hush I told Spot to **hush.**

I told Spot to **keep quiet.** He was barking.

---

hut

This very little house is a **hut.**

a	b	c	d	e
f	g	h	i	j
k	l	m	n	o
p	q	r	s	t
u	v	w	x	y
		z		

I i

I **I** love my mother. I go to school. I have a baby brother. I am happy.

ice

Here is a block of **ice.** When water becomes very cold, it turns to ice.

We use ice to keep food cold and fresh.

When the lake froze, we skated on the ice.

ice cream **Ice cream** is made of milk, eggs, and sugar. Ice cream is frozen. It is sweet and tastes good. Do you like chocolate or strawberry ice cream better?

A dish of ice cream.

An ice cream cone.

if We may not play outdoors **if** it rains. We must play indoors if it rains.

---

ill When I had a bad cold, I was **ill.**

When I had a bad cold, I was **sick.** I was **not well.**

I'll **I'll** means **I will.** Mary wants to know if I'll come to the party.

I'm **I'm** means **I am.** Yes, I'm going to the party.

---

in The blue bird is **in** the cage. The red bird is out of the cage.

My handkerchief is in my pocket.

Peggy lives in the city. Her cousin lives in the country.

---

inch This line is one **inch** long ———.

---

inches One foot is equal to twelve **inches.**

One yard is equal to thirty-six inches.

---

indeed Yes, **indeed,** I am glad. I am really very glad.

Indian Here are some **Indians** long ago. **Indians** were the first Americans. They have lived in this country a very long time. They were here long before other people came.

---

ink We write with pen and **ink.** Ink comes in a bottle.

---

inside

The black mouse is **inside** the box. The white mouse is outside the box.

---

instead Father took his raincoat **instead** of his overcoat. Father took his raincoat **in place of** his overcoat.

interested I am **interested** in the stars. I want to know about them.

---

into

Bill jumped **into** the water.

The fox went into his hole.

---

invite Patty will **invite** me to her party.

Patty will **ask** me **to come** to her party.

invited All my playmates were **invited** to go to the party, too.

---

iron **Iron** is a metal.

Mother will **iron** my clothes.

Mother will **press** my clothes **with an iron.**

An electric **iron.**

An iron kettle.

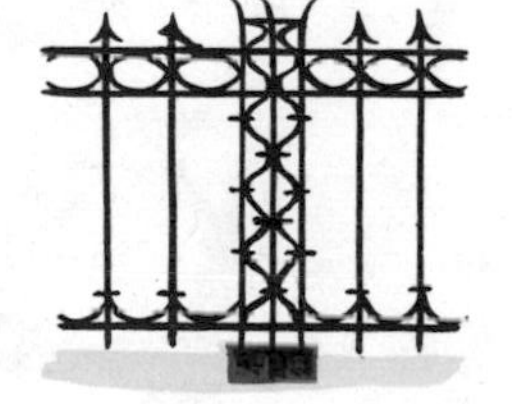

An iron fence.

---

is Jane **is** seven years old today. She is in the second grade this year.

---

island

An **island** is a **piece of land with water all around it.**

We had to go in a boat to reach the island in the lake.

isn't The word **isn't** means **is not.** That isn't the right answer to the question.

---

it John has a baseball glove. His father gave **it** to him.

We are playing tag. I am **it.**

---

its

Mike is watching the rabbit. He is looking at **its** long ears.

---

it's The word **it's** means **it is.** Do you think it's time to go home?

---

itself

The monkey looked at **itself** in a mirror.

My paper doll will stand up **by itself.**

My paper doll will stand up **alone.**

I've **I've** means **I have.** I've had a good time today.

a	*b*	*c*	*d*	*e*
f	*g*	*h*	*i*	*j*
k	*l*	*m*	*n*	*o*
p	*q*	*r*	*s*	*t*
u	*v*	*w*	*x*	*y*
		z		

J j

jacket A **jacket** is a **short coat.** Bobby has a red jacket. He has put an old jacket on the snow man. Bob wears his jacket when he plays in the snow.

jack-o'-lantern We cut holes for eyes, nose, and mouth in a pumpkin. We put a light inside the pumpkin. Then we have a **jack-o'-lantern.**

jail The policeman took the bad man to **jail.** The bad man will be locked up in the jail for a long time.

jam Joe likes strawberry **jam** on his bread. His mother makes jam from fruit.

January **January** is the **first month of the year.** January comes in the winter. It has thirty-one days. New Year's Day is the first day of January.

jar

The glass **jar** is used to hold canned fruit.

The other jar is a cookie jar.

---

jaw My **jaw** is the lower part of my face. My jaw moves when I chew food.

---

jeans **Jeans** are trousers made of strong cotton cloth. Both boys and girls wear them. They are often blue.

---

jelly Mother makes **jelly** of fruit juice and sugar. Most children like jelly on their bread.

---

job

Harry's **job** was to put the wood into a pile.

Harry's **work** was to put the wood into a pile.

---

join We **join** our hands to make a circle.

We **put** our hands **together** to make a circle.

Larry wants to **join** the Boy Scouts. He wants to belong to the Boy Scouts.

joke

The clown fell down and made a loud bang. It was a **joke.** We laughed.

Uncle John told a **joke.**

Uncle John told a **funny story.**

---

jolly Santa Claus is **jolly.**

Santa Claus is **full of fun.**

There was a jolly miller
Lived on the River Dee;
He worked and sang from
morn till night,
No lark so blithe as he.

---

journey I went on a **journey** to see my aunt in another city.

I went on a **trip** to see my aunt in another city.

When I take a journey, I go to a place away from home.

---

joy It was a fine, spring day. The children ran and skipped with **joy.**

The children ran and skipped with **happiness.**

---

juice

I am squeezing the **juice** out of the orange. I will have a glass of orange juice. It is good for me and I like it.

Sometimes I drink tomato juice.

July **July** is the **seventh month of the year.** It has thirty-one days. July is in the middle of the summer. The Fourth of July is sometimes called Independence Day.

---

jump I can **jump** over the box. I can jump a long way if I run first.

I jump in the air and land on my feet.

jumped  The horse **jumped** over the log.

jumping The little boy was **jumping** up and down.

June **June** is the **sixth month of the year.** June comes in the summer. It has thirty days.

January February March April May **June**

---

just My shoes are **just** the right size. They just fit me.

It is **just about** time to go to school.

It is **almost** time to go to school.

Nancy has **just** gone by the house. She went by the house a minute ago.

1	2	3
4	5	6
7	8	9
	10	

K k

kangaroo

A **kangaroo** is a big animal. He can jump a long way. You may see a kangaroo in the zoo.

keep

Mother gave me a ring. I will **keep** it.
I will **have** it **for a long time.**

I will **keep** it safely in the box.
I will **take care of** it safely in the box.

kept I have **kept** my teddy bear since I was a baby.

kettle

We boil water in a **kettle.**
We boil water in a **pot.**

Polly, put the kettle on,
Polly, put the kettle on,
Polly, put the kettle on,
We'll all have tea.

key

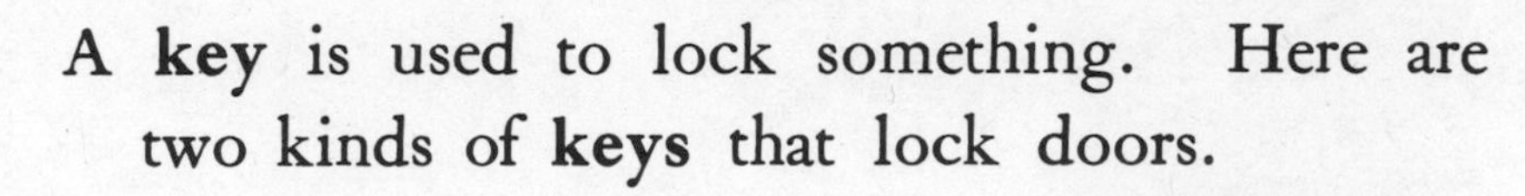

A **key** is used to lock something. Here are two kinds of **keys** that lock doors.

There are also piano **keys.** We strike the piano keys when we play the piano.

---

kick I **kick** the football.

I hit the football **with my foot.**

Sometimes I kick the covers off me at night.

kicked The horse **kicked** at the dog.

---

kid A **kid** is a **baby goat.**

Dan says, "Come on, **kids,** let's play tag."

Dan says, "Come on, **children,** let's play tag."

---

kilometer A **kilometer** is equal to 1,000 meters. Seattle is about 2,800 kilometers from Chicago.

---

kind My big brother is **kind** to us.

My big brother is **gentle and nice** to us.

What **kind** of pie do you like best? What kind of games do you like to play?

kindergarten

In **kindergarten** all the children learn to play and work together. The kindergarten teacher shows them how. Kindergarten is the grade before the first grade. Do you like to have the kindergarten teacher read you a story?

---

king Some countries have a **king.** The king is the head of the people in his country. In our country we do not have a king. We have a president.

The king was in the counting-house
Counting out his money;
The queen was in the parlor
Eating bread and honey.

---

kiss

Mother gave me a **kiss** on my cheek. She pressed her lips against my cheek.

---

kitchen Our family usually eats in the **kitchen.**

Our family usually eats in the **room where our food is cooked.**

kite

A **kite** is made of light wood covered with paper. A kite is carried through the air by the wind. Jim and his sister are flying different kinds of **kites.** They are holding the kites by strings.

---

kitten

A **kitten** is a **young cat.**

A mother cat may have several **kittens.**

---

kitty **Kitty** means **kitten.**

---

knee

I bend one **knee** at a time when I go upstairs. I bend both **knees** when I jump. Baby crawls on his hands and knees.

---

knew **I knew** it was Bill before he took off his false face.

I was sure it was Bill before he took off his false face.

I knew my lesson today.

I had my lesson **in mind** today.

Ralph **knew** all the children on his street.

Ralph **had for friends** all the children on his street.

knife We cut with a **knife.**

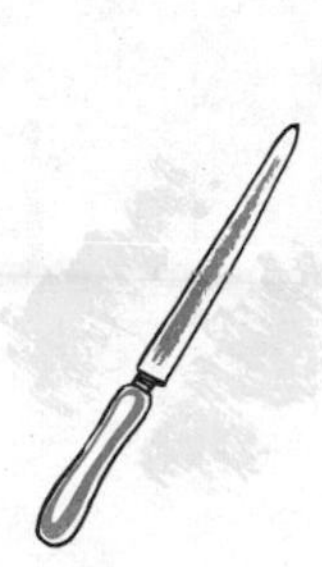

Here is a knife you use at the table.

This is a knife you use in the kitchen.

This knife is called a jackknife.

And this is a hunting knife.

---

knock I will **knock** on the door.

I will **hit** on the door.

knocked I **knocked** the ball to Jim.

---

knot

Can you tie a **knot** like this?

This knot is called a "square knot."

We wrapped the string around the box and tied a knot in it.

---

know I **know** that I am six years old.

I **am sure** that I am six years old.

I **know** a poem.

I **have** a poem **in mind.**

knew I **knew** lots of children at the party.

knows Bill **knows** that I am playing a trick on him.

A B C D E
F G H I J
K L M N O
P Q R S T
U V W X Y
Z

L l

lace  I have **lace** on my handkerchief.

 My shoe **lace** ties my shoe on.
I can **lace** my own shoes. 

lad A **lad** is a **boy.** I read a story about a small lad and a big dog.

ladder We climb a **ladder** to reach high places. Here are tall **ladders.**

lady My mother is a **lady.**
My mother is a **woman.**

lain Nancy has **lain** down to take a nap.

---

lake A **lake** is water with land all around it. In summer we swim in the lake.

lamb

A **lamb** is a **baby sheep.** I saw a mother sheep and two little **lambs.**

Mary had a little lamb,
Its fleece was white as snow;
And everywhere that Mary went
The lamb was sure to go.

---

lamp A **lamp** gives light.

Here is an electric lamp.

Here is a lamp that burns oil.

---

land We walk on the **land.** We swim in the water.
Bob's dog is on land. Bob is in the water.

The farmer is digging in the **land.**
The farmer is digging in the **ground.**

The United States is our **land.**
The United States is the **country we live in.**

The black bird is the last to **land.**
The black bird is the last to **come to the ground.**

lantern

A **lantern** gives light.

A farmer carries a **lantern** at night.

A farmer carries a **light** at night.

Dick carries a lantern when he takes a walk in the country.

---

lap I sit on mother's **lap** when she reads to me. Susie holds the kitty on her lap.

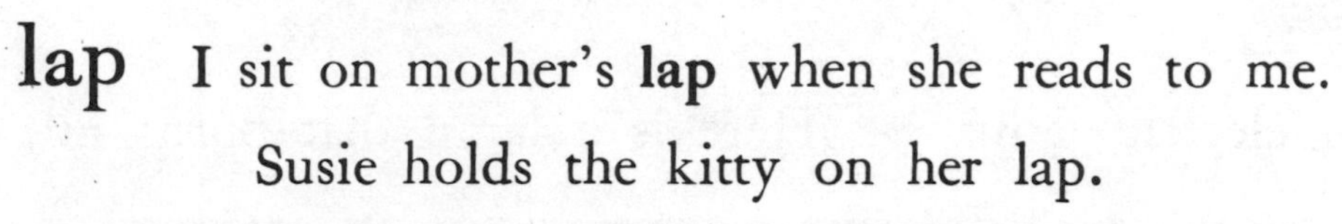

Our kitten can **lap** up milk out of a dish. He laps it with his tongue. This is the way animals drink.

---

large An elephant is **large.**

An elephant is **big.**

larger The elephant is **larger** than a horse. A horse is larger than a dog.

largest The elephant is the **largest** of the three animals.

last 

The black bird is the **last** one to land.

I went to bed early **last** night. Last night was the night before this one.

Halloween is the **last** day in October. There are no more days in October after Halloween.

This movie will **last** two hours.

This movie will **go on** for two hours.

---

late James stayed up too **late** last night. This morning he was sleepy and got up late.

James was **late** for school. He came after time for school to begin. He was **tardy.**

---

later James was late, but Susan was **later.** She came to school after James.

You go to the picnic now. I will come **later.**

I will come **after a while.**

---

laugh Paul has a loud **laugh.**

See the children **laugh!** Something is funny.

laughed When the clowns came out, everybody **laughed** at them.

laughing The children are **laughing** at the dancing bear and the dancing dog.

lawn Joan is cutting the **lawn.**

Joan is cutting the **grass in the yard.**

---

lay Dick will **lay** the book on the table.

Dick will **put** the book **down** on the table.

Chickens **lay** eggs in their nests. Other birds lay eggs, too.

My dog **lay** down yesterday when I told him to. Today he won't lie down.

---

lazy A **lazy** boy is a boy who does not want to work. Anybody who is lazy does not want to work.

---

lead

I will **lead** my pony through the door.

I will **guide** my pony through the door. I will go ahead of him and show him the way.

led Charles **led** his dog.

---

lead **Lead** is a heavy metal. It is like iron.

You write with a **lead** pencil. The lead in the center is soft and black. It is not a metal, but it has the same name as the metal.

---

leader Bob was chosen **leader** of his team. A leader shows other people what to do. A leader tells other people what to do.

leaf A **leaf** is part of a tree or plant.

These are **leaves.**

In autumn the leaves fall from some trees.

Sometimes the page of a book is called a **leaf.**

---

lean

When **I lean** forward over the wash bowl.

When I brush my teeth, **I bend a little** forward over the wash bowl.

When Baby is tired, he will **lean on** Mother.

When Baby is tired, he will **bend and rest against** Mother.

Do you like **lean** meat or fat meat?

---

leap

Watch the frog **leap** into the water.

Watch the frog **jump** into the water.

---

learn I will **learn** to write well.

I will **find out how** to write well.

leather **Leather** is made from the skin of an animal. My shoes are made of leather. Some coats are made of leather. Daddy's belt is made of leather.

---

leave Daddy will **leave** his office at five o'clock.

Daddy will **go away from** his office at five o'clock.

I will **leave** my ball and bat here until tomorrow. I won't take them with me.

left Jack **left** his cap at my house. He went without taking his cap.

---

leaves In the autumn, **leaves** fall from some trees.

Sometimes the pages of a book are called **leaves.**

---

led Charles **led** his dog. He went ahead of his dog and showed him the way.

---

left

I hold up my **left** hand. Which is your left foot?

Jack **left** his cap at my house. He went without taking his cap.

Mother **left** the house a few minutes ago.

Mother **went away from** the house a few minutes ago.

leg

The clown has one **leg** in the air. The little dog has both his back **legs** in the air.

Leg over leg
As the dog went to Dover;
When he came to a stile,
Jump he went over.

A fly has six **legs.**

Beds and tables and chairs have **legs.**

---

lemon

A **lemon** is a fruit. **Lemons** have a sour juice.

---

lemonade I make **lemonade** with lemon juice and sugar and water. Lemonade is a very good drink.

---

length The **length** of the ruler is twelve inches. It is twelve inches from one end of the ruler to the other end. The ruler is twelve inches long.

---

lesson My **lesson** today is on page ten of my book. My lesson is what I am to learn.

let My mother will not **let** me play in the street. If she will not let me, I cannot do it. My mother will let me play in our yard. I can play in our yard.

---

let's **Let's** means **let us.** Let's play with our new puppy.

---

letter

Bill is reading a **letter.** The letter came in the mail this morning.

A is a **letter.** B is a letter. Twenty-six **letters** make up all our words.

---

lettuce **Lettuce** is a leafy vegetable. We grow lettuce in our garden.

The rabbit is eating the lettuce.

---

library A **library** is a place where many books are kept.

---

lick Kitty will **lick** her paws.

Kitty will **wet** her paws **with her tongue.**

I lick the stamp and stick it on the envelope.

Bob says, "I can **lick** Tim." He means, "I can win if I fight Tim."

licked

The dog **licked** the plate clean.

lid The cover on a bucket, a kettle, a can, or a box is called a **lid.** Mother put a lid on the cookie box.

We have **lids** on our eyes. When we close our eyelids, we cannot see.

---

lie I must not tell a **lie.**

I must not tell **something that is not true.**

If I lie, I will be sorry.

If I **say something that is not true,** I will be sorry.

lying The naughty boy is **lying.**

---

lie **I lie** in my bed at night. Sometimes I lie on my side, and sometimes I lie on my back. When I lie in bed I like to be covered with a warm blanket. Don't you?

lain Nancy has **lain** down to take a nap.

lay My dog **lay** down yesterday when I told him to. Today he won't lie down.

lying Bruce is **lying** on his stomach, taking a sun bath.

---

life A plant or an animal or a person has **life.** They all live and grow. A stone does not have life.

An elephant has a long **life.** He lives a long time.

A butterfly has a short life. It lives a short time.

I saved the life of my plant by giving it water.

lift

Robert can **lift** the little pig.

Robert can **take up** the little pig.

Sometimes my mother lets me lift my baby sister. I can lift her and hold her in my arms.

---

light The sun makes **light.** An electric light makes light. When there is light, we can see.

This feather is **light.** It is not heavy.

Yellow is a **light** color. Brown is a dark color.

---

lightning The **lightning** makes a very bright, quick light in the sky.

Lightning and thunder often come when we have a rain storm.

---

like

These two mice look **like** each other.

These two mice look **the same as** each other.

I **like** to play.

I **enjoy** playing.

liked John said he **liked** to eat watermelon.

---

lilies Daddy gave Mother some **lilies** for Easter. Lilies are pretty flowers.

lily

A **lily** is a flower.

---

limb The bird sits on the **limb** of a tree.

The bird sits on the **branch** of a tree.

A leg is sometimes called a **limb**.

---

line This is a **line.** ————————

This is a telephone **line.**

This is a clothes **line.**

And this is a **line** of children.

lion

A **lion** is a wild animal. The lion is called the king of animals because he is so big and strong and fierce. There is a lion in our zoo. When the **lions** roar, it sounds like thunder.

---

lip See my upper **lip**. See my lower lip.

When I open my **lips** you can see my teeth.

---

listen Bob will **listen** on the telephone.

Bob will **try to hear** on the telephone.

listened We **listened** to music on the radio.

---

little

Baby is **little.** Daddy is big.

Little drops of water, little grains of sand,
Make the mighty ocean and the pleasant land.

---

live If I water my plant and keep it in the sun, it will **live** and grow. It will not die.

The birds **live** in a nest. We live in a house.

lived We have **lived** in this house for ten years.

living George Washington is not **living.** He died long ago.

load Steve has brought us a **load** of wood.

I will **load** the wood on my cart and take it to the shed.

---

loaf

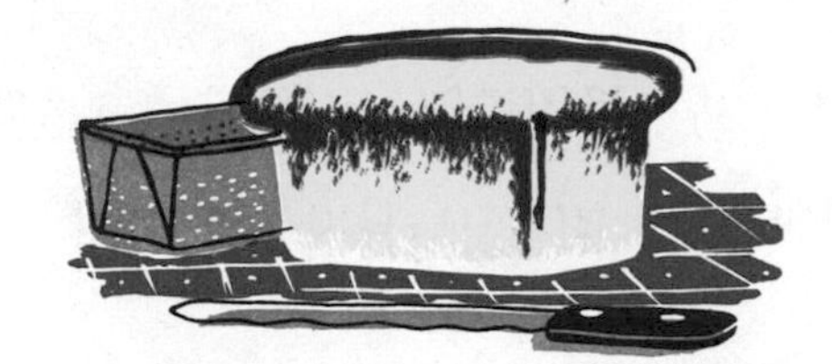

Here is a **loaf** of bread.

---

loaves The baker bakes many **loaves** of bread.

---

lock

This is a **lock**.

This is the lock in our door. You turn the lock with a key.

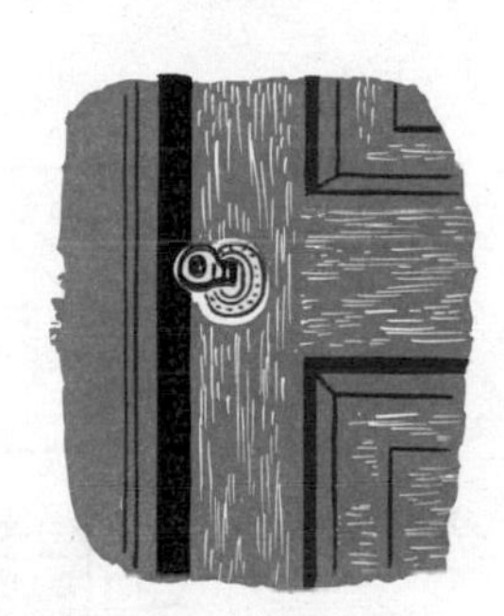

When you leave home, you **lock** all the doors.

locked We **locked** the car when we left it.

---

log

The men cut the tree down. Then they cut it into pieces. Each piece is called a **log**.

long

This is a **long** box. This is a short box.

In the winter the nights are **long.** In the summer the days are long.

Did Cinderella **long** to go to the dance?

Did Cinderella **want very much** to go to the dance?

---

longer

I have waited for Jim a long time, but I will wait a little **longer.**

The red line is **longer** than the black one. ———

---

look

Jerry can **look** out of the window.

Jerry can **try to see** out of the window.

I lost my ball. I will **look for** it.

I will **try to find** it.

People say that **I look** like my mother.

Laura has a happy **look** on her face.

looked I **looked** up in the sky to see the airplane.

looking I am **looking** for my dog. He has run away.

looks Baby **looks** as if he has been in the jam pot.

loose

The wheel on Bob's wagon is **loose.** Mother will fix it. She will fasten it tight.

There is a loose button on your coat. You should sew it on tight.

---

lose I must hold my money tight so that I won't **lose** it. Mother pins my mittens to my snowsuit so that I won't lose them.

lost I **lost** my penny yesterday. I can't find it anywhere.

---

lot

Jack has **a lot** of toys.

Jack has **many** toys.

The men are going to build a store on this **lot.**

The men are going to build a store on this **piece of ground.**

---

loud I can make a **loud** noise with my drum. Thunder makes a loud noise.

---

love Father and Mother **love** their children.

Father and Mother **like** their children **very much.**

loves Baby **loves** Mother. He kisses her because he loves her.

---

lovely Alice is a **lovely** girl.

Alice is a **beautiful and good** girl.

low My mother has a **low** voice.

My mother has a **soft** voice.

The airplane is flying **low.**

The airplane is flying **near the ground.**

This tree has **low** branches.

---

lower

The airplane is flying **lower** and lower. It is going to land.

Please **lower** the window shade.

Please **pull down** the window shade.

---

lump

I have a **lump** on my head where I bumped it.

I have a **swelled place** on my head where I bumped it.

Tommy is going to eat a **lump** of sugar.

Tommy is going to eat a **small piece** of sugar.

A lump of coal.

A lump of dirt.

lunch We eat **lunch** at noon.
We eat **a meal** at noon.

---

lunch basket We carry our picnic lunch in a **lunch basket.**

---

lying

This cow is **lying** down.

This cow is standing up.

---

lying The naughty boy is **lying.**
The naughty boy is **saying things that are not true.**

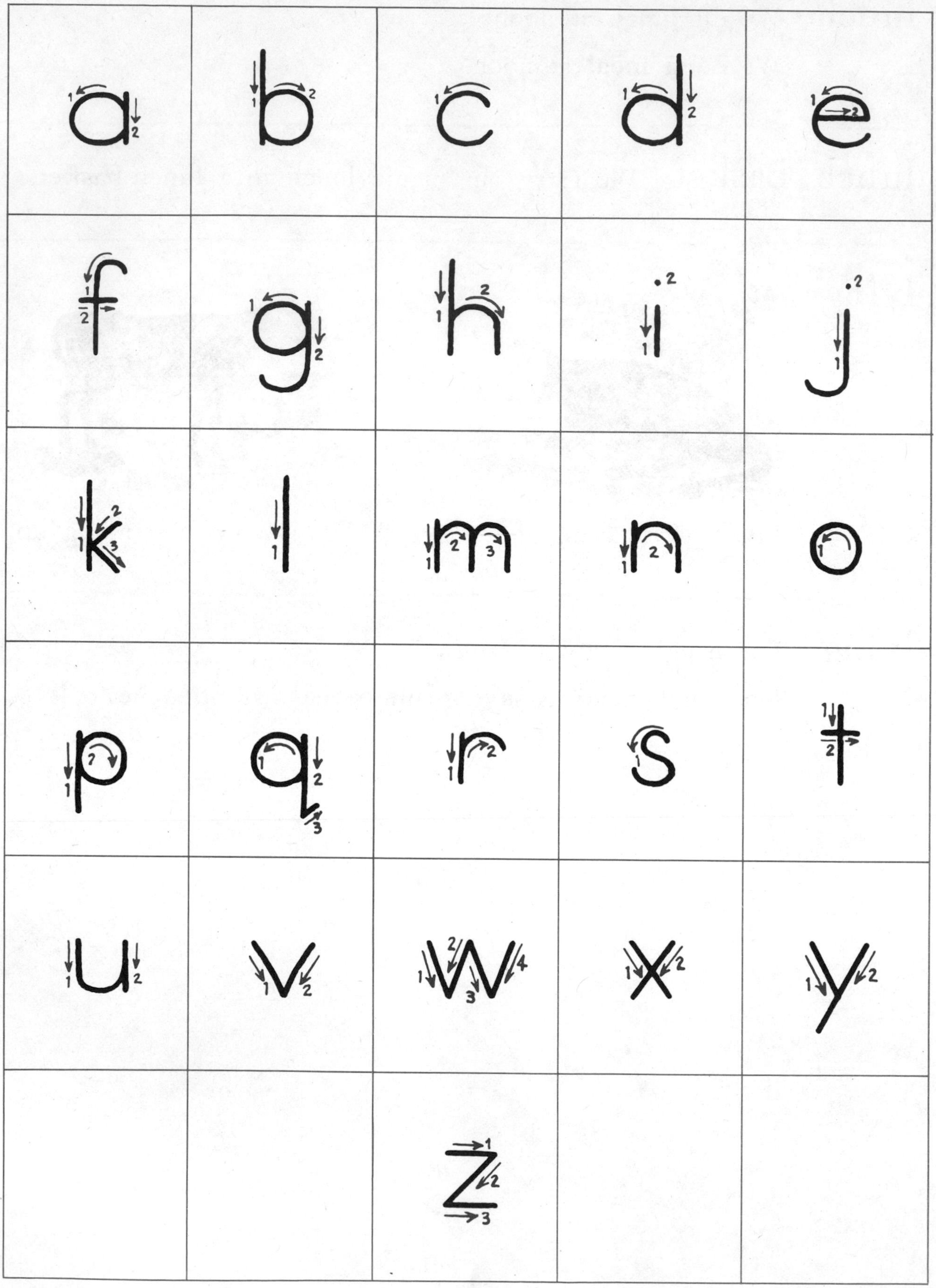

a	b	c	d	e
f	g	h	i	j
k	l	m	n	o
p	q	r	s	t
u	v	w	x	y
		z		

M m

machine A **machine** does work faster than people can do it.

This machine sews.

This machine washes clothes.

This machine is used on the farm.

This machine helps build roads.

This machine saws wood.

This machine sweeps the floor.

This machine is an automobile.

mad Sometimes when we are **angry**, we say, "I'm **mad.**"
We do not go near a **mad** dog. It is very **ill.**

---

made My mother **made** a dress for me.
My mother **sewed** a dress for me.

Freddie **made** a playhouse of tree branches.
Freddie **built** a playhouse of tree branches.

Laura **made** friends wherever she went.
Laura **got** friends wherever she went.

Anne **made** some money by helping her mother.
Anne **earned** some money by helping her mother.

Playing hard **made** me tired.
Playing hard **caused** me **to be** tired.

---

magic The good fairy in the story changed the pumpkin into a coach. This was **magic.** It happens only in stories.

The man in the show pulled a rabbit out of his hat. He said it was **magic,** but it was really a trick.

Do you like to go to a show and see someone do magic tricks? Jerry knows many magic tricks. He can fool his friends.

maid Where are you going, my pretty **maid?**
Where are you going, my pretty **girl?**

We have a **maid** to help with the housework.
We have a **servant girl** to help with the housework.

The maid was in the garden hanging out the clothes;
Along came a blackbird, and snipped off her nose.

---

mail The **mail** came. In the mail were some letters, a package, and a newspaper.

Jack will **mail** the letter.
Jack will **put** the letter **in the mailbox.**

---

mailbox The box that the mail is put into is called the **mailbox.**

---

mail carrier The person who brings the mail is the **mail carrier.** If the person is a man, he is also sometimes called the **mailman.**

main The **main** show was in the big tent.

The **largest and best** show was in the big tent.

---

make

The children can **make** a snowman.

The children can **build** a snowman.

They will make another arm for the snowman after they put on his nose and hat.

Jessie will **make** a dress for her doll.

Jessie will **sew** a dress for her doll.

I expect to **make** many friends at my new school.

I expect to **get** many friends at my new school.

My parents work to **make** money for our family.

My parents work to **earn** money for our family.

Playing hard will **make** you tired.

Playing hard will **cause** you **to be tired.**

made Bob **made** a birdhouse yesterday.

making Father and Jean are **making** a rag rug.

---

mamma **Mamma** is a pet name for mother. Baby loves her mamma.

---

man Daddy is a **man.** James is a boy. James will grow up to be a man like Daddy.

many There are **many** cows in the field.

There are **a large number** of cows in the field.

---

map A **map** shows you where countries and oceans are. It shows you where towns and lakes and rivers are. The map of North America shows the United States. We find our way with a road map when we drive in the car.

---

maple A **maple** is a kind of tree. Have you ever eaten maple sugar? It is made from a juice which comes out of the maple tree.

---

marble  Here is a **marble.** **Marbles** are round and are sometimes made of glass.

The boys are playing a game with marbles.

March **March** is the **third month of the year.** It has thirty-one days.

March comes at the end of winter.

January February **March** April May June

---

march The soldiers **march.**

The soldiers **walk in step with each other.**

A piece of music for people to march to is called a **march.**

mark Susan makes a **mark** on the sidewalk with chalk.

I got a good **mark** on my paper. My mark was 100.

I got a good **grade** on my paper.

Mark an X on the paper.

Write an X on the paper.

---

market

A **market** is a place where people buy things. At this market people buy fruits and vegetables.

To market, to market, to buy a plum bun;
Home again, home again, market is done.

---

marry When a man and a woman **marry,** they **become husband and wife.**

married Father and Mother were **married** in church.

---

master A dog knows his **master.**

A dog knows his **owner.**

mat A small rug is sometimes called a **mat.** We wipe our feet on a door mat.

We put a **mat** under hot dishes when we put them on the table.

---

match  The **match** is burning.

These buttons **match.**

These buttons **are alike.**

These buttons do not match.

These buttons are not alike.

My blue hat will **match** my blue suit.

My blue hat will **go with** my blue suit.

---

matches  We used several **matches** to light the candles.

---

matter What is the **matter?**

What is the **trouble?**

Oh, dear, what can the matter be?
Oh, dear, what can the matter be?
Oh, dear, what can the matter be?
Johnny's so long at the fair.

May **May** is the **fifth month of the year.** It comes in spring. May has thirty-one days. Memorial Day comes in May.

---

may Mother said, "You **may** play with Mary."

Mother said, "You **are allowed to** play with Mary."

We **may** have a picnic tomorrow if the weather is good.

We **will perhaps** have a picnic tomorrow if the weather is good.

might Santa **might** leave me a toy while I am asleep.

---

maybe **Maybe** I can go, but I am not sure.

Perhaps I can go, but I am not sure.

---

me Mother said, "Who wants a dish of ice cream?" My little sister said, "**Me,** me, me!" Mother gave me the bucket of ice cream, and Susie helped me put it in dishes.

---

meadow This field is a **meadow.**

This field is a **place where grass grows.** Sometimes hay grows in a meadow.

---

meal

Breakfast is a **meal.**

Lunch is a meal.

Dinner is a meal.

mean John was **mean** to his dog.

John was **not kind** to his dog.

What do you **mean?**

What do you **have in mind?**

My teacher asks: "What does this poem **mean?** Do you understand it? Do you know what it says?"

---

measure To **measure** means to find out

how long,
how high,

how heavy,

how much,

how many minutes.

---

meat

Meat is a food. It comes from animals. These are some kinds of meat.

We have meat and vegetables for our dinner.

medal Dick's father got a **medal** for being brave in the war. My big brother got a medal for being hurt in the war.

---

medicine

When I am sick, I take **medicine.** The doctor gives me medicine to make me well.

I do not like to be sick. I will take my medicine and get well.

---

meet Susan is going to **meet** Daddy.

Susan is going to **come to** Daddy.

met I **met** the mailman going down the street. Then Bill and I met each other at the corner.

---

melon A **melon** is a large fruit that grows on a vine. It is sweet and juicy inside. One kind of melon is a watermelon.

---

melt Ice begins to **melt** when you hold it in your warm hand. Sugar will melt if you heat it in a pan. Candy will melt when you hold it in your mouth.

melted When the sun began to shine, the snow **melted.** It turned into water.

---

men My father and my grown-up brother are **men.** Boys grow to be men.

mend

This sailor can **mend** the hole in the sail.

Father will **mend** my broken toy.

---

meow A cat says, "**Meow,** meow."

---

merry People are **merry** at Christmas time.

People are **laughing and happy** at Christmas time.

Merry are the bells, and merry would they ring,
Merry was myself and merry would I sing;
With a merry ding-dong, happy, gay, and free,
And a merry sing-song, happy let us be!

---

merry-go-round I like to ride on the **merry-go-round.** I ride on a wooden horse. He goes round and round while the music plays.

---

met Bill and I **met** each other at the corner.

---

metal A **metal** is very hard. Most **metals** are heavy. Iron, lead, silver, and gold are metals.

---

meter A **meter** is about three inches longer than a yard.

mice

Here are some **mice.** One mouse is in the cheese.

When the cat's away,
The mice will play.

---

microphone A **microphone** makes the sound of a voice louder.

People talk into a **microphone** when they broadcast on the radio. The microphone helps to send sounds from the broadcasting station to your radio.

---

middle This x is in the **middle** of the circle.
This x is in the **center** of the circle.

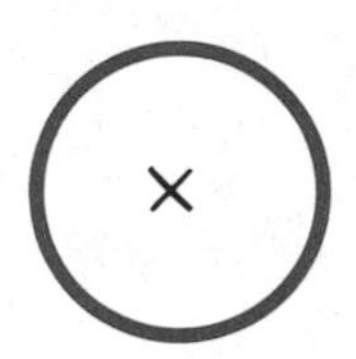

×

This x is in the middle of the square.
This x is in the center of the square.

The yellow bird is in the middle.

---

might Mother said I **might** play with Mary.
Mother said I was **allowed to play** with Mary.

Santa Claus **might** leave me a toy while I am asleep.
Santa Claus **will perhaps** leave me a toy while I am asleep.

mile It takes Jimmy and Sally twenty minutes to walk a **mile.** It is a mile to their school. It is many **miles** to the next town.

---

milk Cows give us **milk.** Milk is good to drink. Cheese is made from milk.

Have you ever seen anyone **milk** a cow?

Milky Way

The **Milky Way** can be seen across the sky at night. There are more stars in the Milky Way than there are people living on the earth.

---

mill Flour is ground from wheat in a flour **mill.**

Cotton is made into cloth in a cotton **mill.**

In this **mill** grandmother ground her coffee.

---

miller The **miller** looks after the flour mill.

Blow, wind, blow, and go, mill, go,
That the miller may grind his corn;
That the baker may take it,
And into bread bake it,
And bring us a loaf in the morn.

mind Your **mind** tells you what to do. You think with your mind. You learn with your mind. You decide with your mind. You know with your mind.

Do you **mind** if we go out to play?

Do you **care** if we go out to play?

Mother says, "Please **mind** me, dear."

Mother says, "Please **obey** me, dear."

Janie will **mind** her dolls.

Janie will **take care of** her dolls.

---

mine The book is **mine.** I own the book. It is not yours, it is mine.

A **mine** is a deep hole in the earth. Coal comes out of a mine. Metal comes out of a mine.

---

minute A **minute** is a measure of time. There are sixty seconds in a minute. There are sixty **minutes** in an hour.

I will be there in a **minute.**

I will be there in a **very short time.**

The clock tells you that it is twenty minutes after eight.

The minutes almost seem to race
When it is growing late;
The very most exciting place
Is just half after eight.

mirror

A **mirror** is a **looking glass.**
Kitty sees herself in the mirror.

Miss Our teacher is **Miss** Brown. She is not married and wants to be called Miss.

---

miss I try to hit the nail with my hammer.

Sometimes **I miss** it.

Sometimes **I do not hit** it.

I was sick and had to **miss** school. I wasn't at school.

My father is away on a trip. **I miss** him. I want him to come home.

Mother says, "Hurry, or you will **miss** the school bus."

Mother says, "Hurry, or you will **not catch** the school bus."

missed

I missed my chance to catch the ball.

---

mistake When you do something wrong without meaning to, it is a **mistake.** I put your cap on by mistake. I thought it was mine.

I made a mistake in writing my name. I did not write every letter in my name.

mitten 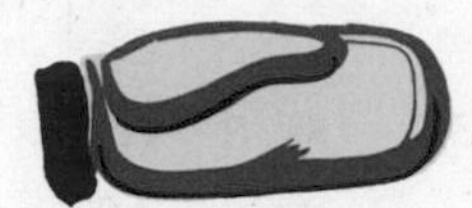 A yellow **mitten.**

Jack has one **mitten** on and one mitten off. Jim has both **mittens** on. They keep his hands warm.

The three little kittens
Found their mittens,
And they began to cry,
"Oh! Mother dear, see here, see here,
Our mittens we have found."

---

mix Sometimes I **mix** flour and water to make paste.

Sometimes I **stir together** flour and water to make paste.

The children **mix** their mother up when they ask her to do so many things at once. She doesn't know what she is doing.

---

moment I will be there in a **moment.**

I will be there in a **very short time.**

Monday **Monday** is the **second day of the week.**

Sunday **Monday** Tuesday Wednesday Thursday Friday Saturday

money A half-dollar is **money.** A quarter is money. A dime is money. A dollar bill is paper money. You pay for things with money.

My mother gives me a dime to spend on candy. I earn money when I work.

If I'd as much money as I could spend,
I never would cry old chairs to mend;
If I'd as much money as I could tell,
I never would cry old clothes to sell.

---

monkey

A **monkey** is a funny animal. Have you seen **monkeys** at the zoo? I like to watch them play together. They hang by their tails and leap through the air.

Sometimes Daddy says, "Don't **monkey with** that."
Sometimes Daddy says, "Don't **touch or play with** that."

---

month A **month** is a part of a year. There are twelve **months** in a year. They are January, February, March, April, May, June, July, August, September, October, November, December.

Mm

moo The cow says, "**Moo,** moo."

---

moon

We see the **moon** shining at night.

The Man in the Moon looked out of the moon,
Looked out of the moon and said,
"'Tis time for all children on the earth
To think about getting to bed."

---

moonlight When the moon shines at night, we have **moonlight.** Moonlight is not as bright as sunshine.

---

more I was tired, but my sister was **more** tired than I was.

Barbara said, "I want **more** milk." Charles said, "I want more cake." Spot begged for more meat. Mother gave them each some more.

---

morning The **first part of the day** is **morning.** The sun is coming up. It is morning. I wake up in the morning and eat my breakfast. Mary and John go to school in the morning. I brush my teeth carefully every morning.

mosquito This is a **mosquito.** It can bite people.

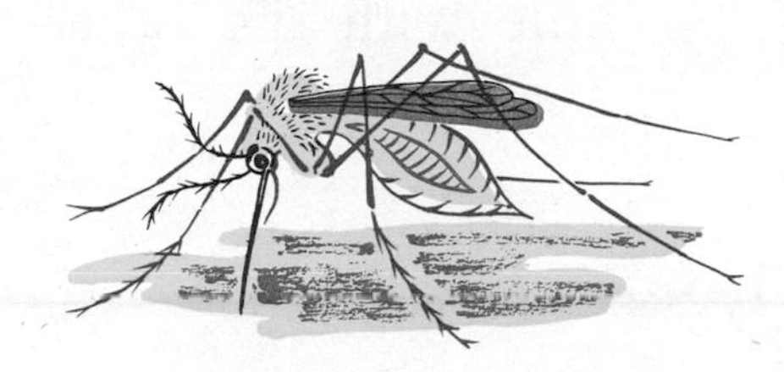

---

most These dolls are beautiful, but this doll is the **most** beautiful of all.

When you divide the cake, give Mother the **most.**

When you divide the cake, give Mother the **largest part.**

John had **most** of the apples.

John had **nearly all** of the apples.

---

mother I love my **mother.** My mother takes care of me. She is married to my father. My mother and father are husband and wife.

---

mountain A **mountain** is a very big hill. These are **mountains.**

When we drove to the country we saw a big mountain.

mouse

This is a **mouse.** He lives in a hole with the other **mice.**

---

mouth I eat and talk with my **mouth.**

This man has a pipe in his mouth.

---

move Will you **move** the table for me?

Will you **put** the table **in a different place** for me?

We will **move** soon.

We will **go to a different place** soon.

moved **I moved** the table for her.

moving These men are **moving** our furniture. We are going to another place to live.

---

moving picture You go to the **moving picture** show to see Mickey Mouse. A moving picture is often called a movie.

Mr. My father is Mister Smith. This is the way to write it: **Mr.** Smith.

Mrs. My mother writes her name this way: **Mrs.** R. J. Smith. She writes Mrs. because she is a married woman.

Ms. Some women use **Ms.** before their names. They may be married or not married. They do not use Miss or Mrs.

---

much How **much** money do you have? How much is left of the cake? I don't like this book very much. Do you have much time to help me?

---

mud **Dirt and water together** make **mud.** My shoes got dirty in the mud.

---

muddy

Bill's rubbers are **muddy.** He has been walking in the mud.

---

music John sings. That is **music.** Mary plays the piano. That is music. A band makes music.

Ride a cock-horse to Banbury Cross,
To see a white lady ride on a white horse!
Rings on her fingers and bells on her toes,
She shall have music wherever she goes.

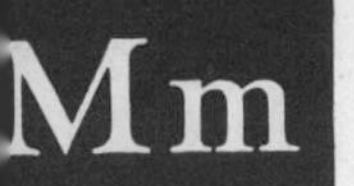

must You **must** drink your orange juice.

You **have to** drink your orange juice.

---

my See **my** pencil. It belongs to me. It is not your pencil.

---

myself I saw the rabbit **myself.**

I hurt **myself** when I fell down.

I don't like to walk to school **by myself.**

I don't like to walk to school **alone.**

A	B	C	D	E
F	G	H	I	J
K	L	M	N	O
P	Q	R	S	T
U	V	W	X	Y
		Z		

a	b	c	d	e
f	g	h	i	j
k	l	m	n	o
p	q	r	s	t
u	v	w	x	y
		z		

N n

nail Robert is holding a **nail** in his hand. He is going to drive it into the wood with a hammer.

I have a **nail** on each finger and each toe. They are my fingernails and toenails.

name My **name** is Sally Brown. What name did your father and mother give you? What is your last name?

What is the **name** of that tree? It is called an oak tree. Oak is its name.

What did you **name** your puppy?

named We **named** the puppy Chips.

nap

Father was sleepy.

He had a **nap** in his chair.

He had a **short sleep** in his chair.

---

napkin Betty is wiping her mouth with a **napkin.**

I have a napkin by my plate at the dinner table.

---

narrow

The path we walked on was **narrow.**

The path we walked on was **not wide.** The street is wide, but the sidewalk is narrow.

---

naughty Jack was a **naughty** boy.

Jack was a **bad** boy.

---

navy A **navy** is all the fighting ships of a country and the men that run them. My uncle is in the navy. The men in the navy are called sailors. Our navy fights on the sea when we are at war.

near

The horse is **near** the fence, but far away from the tree.

The horse is **close to** the fence, but far away from the tree.

---

nearly Mary is **nearly** as tall as her mother.

Mary is **almost** as tall as her mother.

It is nearly time to go to bed.

---

neat Helen keeps her room **neat.**

Helen keeps her room **clean and in order.**

Do you try to keep your room and your clothes neat?

---

neck

Sister is putting the beads around her **neck.** Your head is above your neck. Your shoulders are below your neck.

---

necktie Daddy wears a **necktie** around his neck.

This is a bow tie.

need I **need** a knife to cut the string.

I **should have** a knife to cut the string.

I **need** your help.

I **must have** your help.

needed I was cold. I **needed** my coat to keep me warm.

---

needle

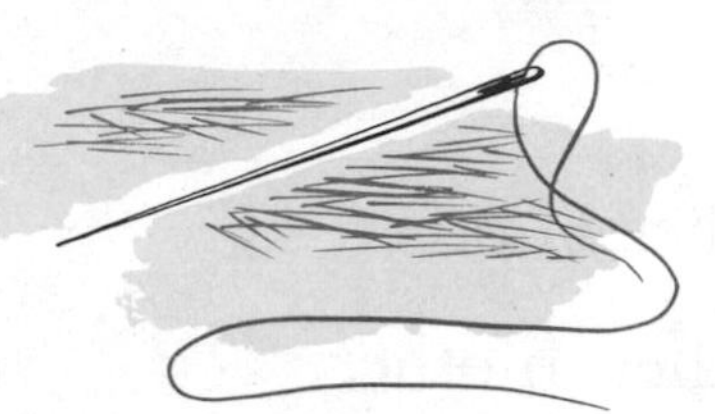

We sew with a **needle** and thread. A needle has a tiny hole in it. The thread goes through the hole.

---

neighbor The **person who lives near me** is my **neighbor.** John lives on a farm near our farm. He is my neighbor.

How do you do neighbor?
Neighbor how do you do?
Very well I thank you.
How does Cousin Sue do?

---

neither Both Tom and Joe ran in the race, but **neither** of them won.

Both Tom and Joe ran in the race, but **not either one** of them won.

The arrow went **neither** to the right nor the left. It went straight to the center of the tree trunk.

---

nephew My Aunt Grace calls me **nephew.** I am her brother's son. Uncle Ray, her husband, calls me **nephew,** too.

nest

The mother bird lays her eggs in a **nest.** The little birds live there while they are learning to fly.

net We use a **net** to keep away flies and bugs.

This is a tennis **net.**

A **net** for catching butterflies.

never I can **never** jump that high.

I can **not ever** jump that high.

new

Joan has a **new** coat. George has an old coat.

I will go to a **new** school when we move.

I will go to a **different** school when we move.

news Father reads the **news** in the paper.

Father reads the **story of what has happened** in the paper.

We all heard the news on the radio.

newspaper

We read the news in a **newspaper.** A newspaper has pictures in it. It has comics in it, too.

New Year's Day **New Year's Day** is the **first day of January.** It is the first day of the year.

---

next

These blocks are not **next** to each other.

My turn is **next.**

My turn is **after this one.**

Now they are next to each other.

Now they are beside each other.

---

nice Our house is **nice.** It is pretty and pleasant to live in. My clothes are nice. They are clean and look well on me. My toys are nice. They are fun to play with.

---

nickel A **nickel** is money. A nickel will buy five cents' worth.

---

niece My Uncle Jack calls me **niece.** I am his sister's daughter. Aunt Nell, his wife, calls me **niece**, too.

---

night At **night** it is dark. During the day it is light. At night I go to bed. I sleep most of the night.

nightgown

Mary wears a **nightgown** to bed.

Mary wears a **night dress** to bed.

Wee Willie Winkie runs through the town,
Upstairs and downstairs, in his nightgown;
Rapping at the window, crying at the lock,
"Are the babies in their beds, for now it's eight o'clock."

---

nine

There are **nine** birds here. Can you count them?

1 2 3 4 5 6 7 8 9 10

---

no Jack had **no** gloves.

Jack had **not any** gloves.

I asked father if I could go swimming. He said, "**No,** it's too cold today."

---

nobody I heard something in the room, but **nobody** was there.

I heard something in the room, but **no person** was there.

---

nod I **nod** when someone asks me a question. I move my head down and up. I mean "Yes."

Sometimes when Grandfather is sleepy, his head will **nod.**

noise

The pans fell down.
They made a loud **noise.**
They made a loud **sound.**

When you know how to play the piano, you can make music. When you don't know how, you pound it, and that is **noise.**

---

none We looked for flowers. There were **none.**
There were **not any.**

---

noon We go to lunch at **noon.**
We go to lunch at **twelve o'clock in the middle of the day.**

---

nor Jim had neither his coat **nor** his cap on.

---

north Point your right hand to where the sun comes up. Point your left hand to where the sun goes down. Look straight ahead. You will be looking toward the **north.** On a map, north is at the top.

---

nose Ellen has a pretty **nose.** She breathes through her nose. She smells with her nose.

The anteater is an animal with a very long nose.

not Joyce will go to the movies. Baby will **not** go to the movies.
Baby is not going to the movies because she is too young.

---

note Mary and I wrote a **note** of thanks.
Mary and I wrote a **short letter** of thanks.

Mother **made a note of** what she needs to buy.
Mother **wrote down** what she needs to buy.

---

nothing

Paul opened the box.
There was **nothing** in it.
There was **not a thing** in it.

---

notice Cinderella did not **notice** that it was midnight.
Cinderella did not **see** that it was midnight.

November **November** is the **eleventh month of the year.** It comes in the autumn. It has thirty days. Thanksgiving comes in November.

Thirty days hath September,
April, June and November,
February has twenty-eight alone,
All the rest have thirty-one;
Excepting leap year, that's the time
When February's days are twenty-nine.

---

now The bell is ringing **now.**
The bell is ringing **at this time.**

number A **number** tells how many. I have one dog. I have two sisters. I have twenty books. One, two, and twenty, are **numbers.**

Here are the numbers from 1 to 10.

1 2 3 4 5 6 7 8 9 10

This is the **number** on our house—421. The number is part of our address. We live at 421 Main Street.

---

nurse

A **nurse** takes care of sick people. A nurse took care of me when I was in the hospital.

---

nut The meat of a **nut** is good to eat. **Nuts** have hard shells and grow on trees. These are nuts.

a	*b*	*c*	*d*	*e*
f	*g*	*h*	*i*	*j*
k	*l*	*m*	*n*	*o*
p	*q*	*r*	*s*	*t*
u	*v*	*w*	*x*	*y*
		z		

oak An **oak** is a kind of tree.

Then here's to the oak, the brave old oak,
Who stands in his pride alone!
And still flourish he, a hale green tree,
When a hundred years are gone!

---

oatmeal I eat **oatmeal** for breakfast. It is made from oats. My mother cooks it for us.

---

oats The **oats** are growing in the field. The grains from oats are used for food. Oats are a very good food for horses.

---

obey I **obey** my parents. I do what they say I am to do. I taught my dog to obey me. He does what I tell him to do.

---

ocean The **ocean** is the largest body of water there is. Ships travel on the ocean.

The **Atlantic Ocean** touches the east shore of America.
The **Pacific Ocean** touches the west shore of America.

o'clock

It is ten **o'clock.**

It is ten **by the clock.**

October **October** is the tenth month of the year. It comes in the autumn. October has thirty-one days. Halloween is the last day in October.

---

of The city **of** New York is very large.

Most **of** the children were playing outdoors.

The skirt **of** my blue dress is too short.
The skirt **that belongs to** my blue dress is too short.

The stories **of** Louisa May Alcott are interesting to children.
The stories **by** Louisa May Alcott are interesting to children.

The big hill is a mile north **of** town.
The big hill is a mile north **from** town.

The king's crown **of** gold is heavy.
The king's crown **made from** gold is heavy.

He was a man **of** good sense.
He was a man **having** good sense.

Tell me the story **of** little Red Riding Hood.
Tell me the story **about** little Red Riding Hood.

It is ten minutes **of** nine.
It is ten minutes **before** nine.

off

The rider got **off** the horse. Then he took his hat off.

When I go to bed, I turn my light **off.**

---

office

This is a post **office.** We mail letters here.

This is an **office.** People work here.

---

often **Often** means **many times.**

I often go downtown. Sometimes I go once a week.

I wash my hands often. Sometimes I wash them ten times a day.

---

oh Betty said, "**Oh,** oh!" She was surprised to see the beautiful Christmas tree.

---

oil

I will **oil** my bicycle with my oil can.

At the filling station they put **oil** in the car.

old

Grandmother is **old.** She has white hair.

I am six years **old.**

I am six years **of age.** In two years I will be as old as my brother is now. I am old enough to go to school.

My brown shoes are too **old** to wear. I got some new ones.

---

older My brother is eight years old. He is **older** than I am.

---

oldest My sister is the **oldest** child in our family. She is twelve years old.

---

on

Where is the doll? It is **on** a chair. The Kitty is on her pillow.

When are you going to the circus? Are you going **on** Tuesday?

How did Larry happen to break the cup? Did he do it **on** purpose?

What is your book about? It looks like a book **on** birds.

The lights were off, but Mother turned them **on.**

I will go **on** reading the story until I finish it.

Oo

once I have seen a wild bear only **once.**

I have seen a wild bear only **one time.**

All the children spoke **at once.**

All the children spoke **at the same time.**

Once upon a time there was a king who had three daughters.

A long time ago there was a king who had three daughters.

---

one 1 A man has **one** nose, one mouth, and one head.

This is the number one—1.

1 2 3 4 5 6 7 8 9 10 11 12

One should be careful when crossing the street.

A person should be careful when crossing the street.

---

one hundred 100 There are **one hundred** cents in a dollar.

There are **100** cents in a dollar.

---

onion

An **onion** is a vegetable. When you peel **onions,** tears come from your eyes. These are different kinds of onions.

---

only This is the **only** road up the mountain. There is no other road up the mountain.

I have **only** one penny.

I have **just** one penny and no more.

Jack is an **only** child. He has no brothers or sisters.

open

The door is **open.**

The door is **not closed.**

I will **open** the box.

I will **take the cover off** the box.

opened The box has been **opened.**

---

or Do you want to play outdoors **or** indoors? Do you want milk or water to drink? Are you going to come home Monday or Tuesday? Do you want a kitty or a puppy?

---

orange

An **orange** is a fruit. We drink orange juice for breakfast.

My mother squeezes the **oranges** to make orange juice.

The color **orange** was named for the fruit.

---

order

These blocks are in **order** by size.

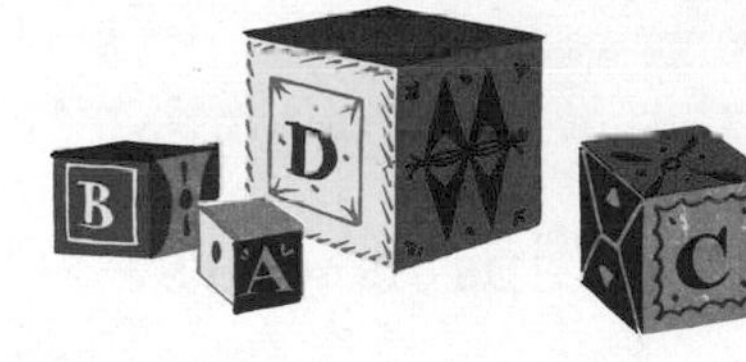

These blocks are not in order by size.

My room is in **order.** Everything is in the right place.

The captain gave the soldiers an **order.** He told them what they had to do.

Mother can call up the store and **order** things. She tells what she wants to buy.

other I will wear the **other** coat today.

I will wear a **different** coat today.

Have you any **other** marbles?

Have you any **more** marbles?

I stayed home and all the **other** children went to the movies.

I stayed home and all the **rest of** the children went to the movies.

George ran up every **other** step.

George ran up every **second** step.

---

ouch I hurt my finger. I said, "**Ouch!**"

---

ought We **ought to** help Mother.

We **should** help Mother. It's the right thing to do.

---

our Chips is **our** dog. He belongs to us.

---

ours Chips is **ours.** The big dog is yours.

---

ourselves We have a playhouse. We fixed it up **ourselves.**

Sally and I have tired **ourselves** out by playing hard.

My brother and I were standing **by ourselves** away from the others.

My brother and I were standing **alone** away from the others.

out

Fido is coming **out** of his house.

Mother wasn't home. I told the man at the door, "My mother is **out.**" I went out with Bill and we played baseball with the boys.

When the lights were **out,** the room was dark. We turn the lights out every night.

---

outdoors The trees are **outdoors.** We are inside our house. We like to play outdoors. We do our school work indoors.

---

outside

Some toys are in the box. One is **outside** on the floor.

The **outside** of the box is colored red. The inside of the box is colored yellow.

Sometimes people say **outside** when they mean **outdoors.**

The outside of our house is painted white. The outside of Ruth's house is red brick.

---

oven My mother cooks food in the **oven.** She takes the bread out of the oven when it is baked. Nancy and her mother baked some cookies in the oven.

over

Betsy is jumping **over** the pool of water.

Betsy is jumping **across** the pool of water.

Doug holds the umbrella **over** his head.

Doug holds the umbrella **above** his head.

The party is **over,** and we must go home.

The party is **at an end,** and we must go home.

Be careful of the tall lamp or you will tip it **over.**

There is snow all **over** the ground.

My sister had to write the letter **over** and over.

My sister had to write the letter **again** and again.

Daddy has **over** five dollars.

Daddy has **more than** five dollars.

---

overalls I wear **overalls** when I play. I am going to put on my overalls now.

---

owl

An **owl** is a bird with big eyes. "Too-hoo," says the owl. **Owls** fly at night.

own This book is my **own.** It belongs to me. The other is a library book. It does not belong to me. It is not my own.

I **own** twelve books.

I **have** twelve books that belong to me.

owned John **owned** five rabbits.

---

ox An **ox** is an animal that looks something like a cow. The heavy cart is pulled by an ox.

---

oxen When one ox and another ox pull together we say, "This is a team of **oxen.**"

1	2	3
4	5	6
7	8	9
	10	

P p

pack

This man carries a **pack** on his back.
This man carries a **bundle** on his back.
He is going to camp in the woods.

The men **pack** the tomatoes in boxes.
The men **put** the tomatoes in boxes.

I **pack** my suitcase when I go away.

package

Mother is giving me a **package.** The package is wrapped. I hope it is a gift. She has other **packages** from the store.

paddle

Daddy pushes his canoe through the water with a **paddle.**
This is the kind of paddle he uses.

page

I am writing my name on the first **page** of my book. I will be careful when I turn each page of my book.

There are many **pages** in this book. Most of the pages have pretty pictures. Do you like to turn the pages and look at the pictures?

---

paid My mother **paid** me for cutting the lawn.

My mother **gave** me **money** for cutting the lawn.

---

pail We carry water in a **pail.** At the lake I fill the pail with sand. A pail is also called a bucket.

Jack and Jill went up the hill
To fetch a pail of water.
Jack fell down and broke his crown,
And Jill came tumbling after.

---

pain When you have a **pain,** some part of your body hurts. My father has a pain in his head. He has a headache. A toothache is a pain in a tooth.

paint

There are many different colors of **paint.** I have a can of red paint.

I will **paint** my wagon red.

I will **color** my wagon red **with paint.**

painted Helen **painted** a picture. She used many colors of paint.

painting My mother is **painting** the baby's high chair.

---

pair A **pair** is **two of a kind.** Here is a pair of shoes. They are two shoes made to be worn by the same person.

This is a pair of gloves.

---

palace

The king lived in a **palace.**

The king lived in a **large and beautiful house.**

pan

My mother is baking a cake in a **pan.**
Pans may hold water or food.

There are different kinds of pans.

---

pancake A **pancake** is flat and round. It is made of milk, eggs, and flour. Bill likes **pancakes.**

---

pansies I saw a bed of flowers of many colors.
They were **pansies.**

---

pansy

A **pansy** is a flower.

---

pant My dog will **pant** if he is too hot.
My dog will **breathe fast** if he is too hot.

pants

Jack is putting on a pair of **pants.** Pants are also called trousers.

---

papa **Papa** is a pet name for **father.**

---

paper The book you are reading now is made of **paper.** We wrap packages in wrapping paper. Wall paper is used to cover the walls of rooms. We write letters on writing paper.

---

parachute

A man uses a **parachute** when he wants to jump out of an airplane. The parachute is fastened to his body. It opens out when he jumps. The parachute makes him float down to the ground slowly.

parade A circus sometimes has a **parade.** Animals and people walk in a circus parade. Sometimes soldiers have a parade. They march past the general.

pardon When you say, "I beg your **pardon,**" you mean, "I am sorry I did that. I didn't mean to." "Pardon me" is the same as "I beg your pardon."

---

park

The **park** has beautiful trees and green lawns. We often take a walk in the park. Ted and I like to feed the birds in the park.

Father will **park** the car here.

Father will **put** the car here.

---

part A **part** of this pie is on the plate.

A **piece** of this pie is on the plate. The whole pie is not in the pan.

The whole of anything is made of its **parts.** The whole of your body is made of its parts. There are many parts to a watch.

Larry likes to **part** his hair on the left side.

---

party

On my birthday I had a **party.** All my friends came to the party.

We played games and had ice cream and cake to eat.

pass The auto will **pass** the bus.

The auto will **go on by** the bus.

Please **pass** me the meat.

Please **hand** me the meat.

The clouds will soon **pass,** and the sun will shine again.

The clouds will soon **move on,** and the sun will shine again.

I work hard in school so that I will **pass.**

I work hard in school so that I will **go on to the next grade.**

passed The parade **passed** our house.

---

past It is **past** one o'clock.

It is **after** one o'clock.

Winter is **past.** It is now spring.

Winter has **gone by.** It is now spring.

---

paste

Paste is used to stick paper together. You can make a kind of paste by mixing flour and water.

Jane likes to **paste** pictures in a book.

Jane likes to **stick** pictures in a book **with paste.**

pasture

The horses are eating grass in the **pasture.**

---

pat Bruce will **pat** his dog.

Bruce will **strike** his dog **gently with his open hand.** This tells the dog that Bruce likes him.

---

patch Mother sewed a **patch** on the knee of my snow pants. The patch covers a hole that I tore in it.

---

patches A patchwork quilt is a bed cover made of **patches.**

A wandering minstrel I—
A thing of shreds and patches.

---

path There is a **path** to the house. It is the place where people walk to the house. There are many pretty **paths** through the woods.

paw

The **foot of an animal with claws** is called a **paw.** Kitty is licking her paw. Cats and dogs have four **paws.** Many other animals have paws.

---

pay

Every week Daddy gets his **pay.**

Every week Daddy gets his **money for working.**

James will **pay** for the chewing gum.

James will **give money** for the chewing gum.

paid My mother **paid** me for cutting the lawn.

---

peach

A **peach** is a fruit. It is yellow and juicy.

---

peaches

May we have **peaches** for supper?

---

peanut

A **peanut** is a plant.

The seeds grow in shells under the ground. We eat the seeds.

These are **peanuts.**

pear

A **pear** is a fruit. It grows on a pear tree. Would you rather have a peach or a pear?

I had a little nut-tree, nothing would it bear
But a silver nutmeg and a golden pear;
The King of Spain's daughter came to visit me,
And all was because of my little nut-tree.
I skipped over water, I danced over sea,
And all the birds in the air couldn't catch me.

---

peas Green **peas** are one of the vegetables I like best. They are really the seeds of the pea plant.

---

peck Watch the chicken **peck** at its food.

Watch the chicken **strike at and pick up** its food.

The woodpecker can **peck** a hole in the bark of a tree.

---

peel Mother will **peel** the apple for me.

Mother will **take off the skin** of the apple for me.

---

peep Baby will **peep** through her fingers if I say, "Peek-a-boo."

Baby will **look** through her fingers if I say, "Peek-a-boo."

Little chicks say, "**Peep,** peep."

II Read the passage and then complete the chart, which organizes some important points from the passage.

The food pyramid is divided into four levels, each representing the ideal amount from that food group. At the bottom, there are grains. This means that you should eat lots of bread, cereal, rice and pasta. Next, you should eat plenty of fruits and vegetables. Then in smaller portions, include meats and dairy foods in your diet. Meats and dairy foods provide proteins; however, you don't need many servings. At the tip of the pyramid are fats and sugars, which you should eat only in small amounts.

The Food Guide Pyramid

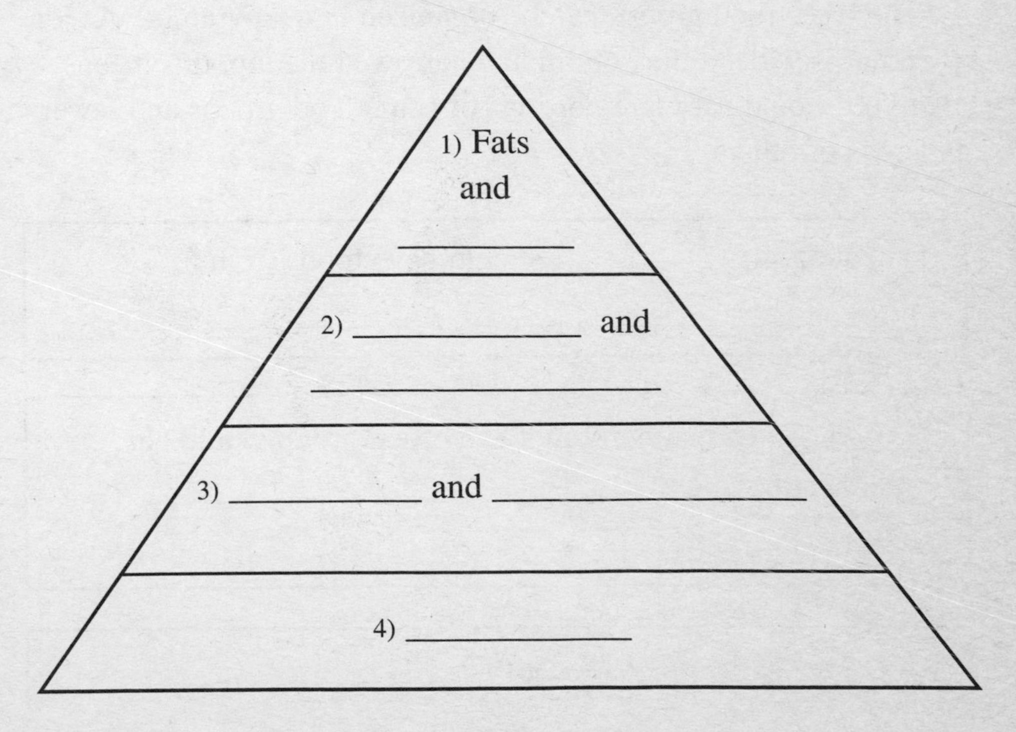

EI 114a

Name: ____________________ Date: / / Time: : ~ :

100%	~90%	~80%	~70%	69%~
(mistakes) 0	-	1	2	3~

1 Read the passage and then complete the main idea of each paragraph.

Diet experts advise you to plan your daily menu around the four basic food groups. These food groups are grains, fruits and vegetables, meat and dairy, and fats and sugars.

However, you should not eat an equal portion of each food group. That would be unhealthy. For example, eating an equal amount of sweets and vegetables would lead to an unbalanced diet.

The basic food groups can be organized into a pyramid. As a pyramid is wide at the bottom and narrow at the top, this means that you should eat more portions of some food groups and fewer portions of others.

1) Your daily __________ should have foods from

____________________________________.

↓

2) Eating an equal portion of each food group would be unhealthy and ____________________________

____________________________.

↓

3) Organize the basic food groups ____________________

________________.

pen

Andy writes with a **pen**

Mary draws with a pencil.

The farmer keeps his pigs in a **pen.**
The farmer keeps his pigs in a **small fenced yard.**

---

pencil Robert can write with a **pencil.** Mary has three **pencils.** Would you rather write with a pencil or a pen?

---

pennies What can you buy with five **pennies?**
What can you buy with five **cents?** Five pennies are worth a nickel.

---

penny A **penny** is a **cent.** What can you buy with a penny?

Hot-cross buns!
Hot-cross buns!
One a penny, two a penny,
Hot-cross buns!

---

people Many **people** were at the movie.
Many **persons** were at the movie.

perfect Bill's spelling paper was **perfect.**

Bill's spelling paper **had no mistakes.** He spelled all the words in the right way.

Will you pick me a **perfect** peach?

Will you pick me a peach that **has nothing wrong with it?**

---

perhaps I think **perhaps** I shall get a letter.

I think **it may be** that I shall get a letter.

---

person I am a **person.** You are a person. Everyone is a person.

---

pet

A **pet** is an **animal that you take care of and play with.** Sam has three **pets.** They are a dog, a monkey, and a pony.

Do you have a pet? What kind of a pet is it? I have a small painted turtle and a bird.

---

piano A **piano** makes music. To play the piano you strike the keys. Our teacher plays the piano when we sing. Bob is learning to play the piano.

pick

John will **pick** the apples.

John will **pull off** the apples **with his fingers.**

Which children do you **pick** to play on your team?

Which children do you **choose** to play on your team?

picked We **picked** a bunch of flowers for Mother.

---

picnic A **picnic** is a party out of doors. We had a picnic in the woods.

At the picnic we had a lunch that we ate under a tree.

We took sandwiches and milk for our picnic lunch. Our family likes to go on a picnic. We always have fun.

---

picture

Lucy is looking at the **picture** of a ship that hangs on our wall. I saw a picture of our President in the newspaper. Would you like to have your picture taken? Jerry has a picture book. It is full of **pictures.**

pie

Mother is cutting a **pie.** She baked three **pies.** They are apple pies.

---

piece I would like a **piece** of the chocolate cake.

I would like a **part** of the chocolate cake. Are there enough **pieces** so that I can have one?

---

pig A **pig** is a **young hog.** Have you ever seen a little pig with its mother? There are many little **pigs** on our farm.

A long-tailed pig or a short-tailed pig,
Or a pig without e'er a tail,
A sow-pig, or a boar-pig,
Or a pig with a curly tail.

---

pile

A **pile** of sand.

A pile of wood.

A pile of boxes.

We will rake the leaves in our back yard. When we make a big pile of leaves we will jump in it.

pillow

A **pillow** is a **bag filled with feathers.** My doll has a small pillow. I have a big pillow. We each have our own **pillows.**

---

pilot A **pilot** of an airplane is the person who makes it fly.
A ship's **pilot** keeps the ship on her course.

---

pin A **pin** is used to fasten things together.

Here are straight **pins.**

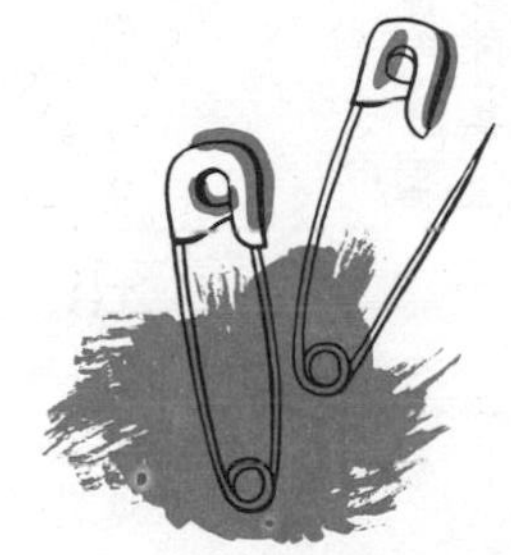

Here are safety pins.

Here is a pin you wear on your dress or coat.

I will **pin** a flower on you.
I will **fasten** a flower on you **with a pin.**

---

pine

A **pine** tree is green all the year round. The leaves of a pine tree are called needles. A pine cone is the fruit of the pine tree. Many pine trees are called a forest of **pines.**

pink 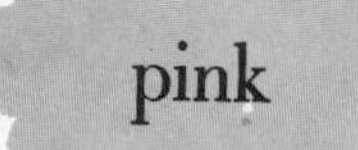 This color is **pink**.

These flowers are pink.

---

pint There are two cups in a **pint**. I was so hungry that I drank a pint of milk.

---

pipe 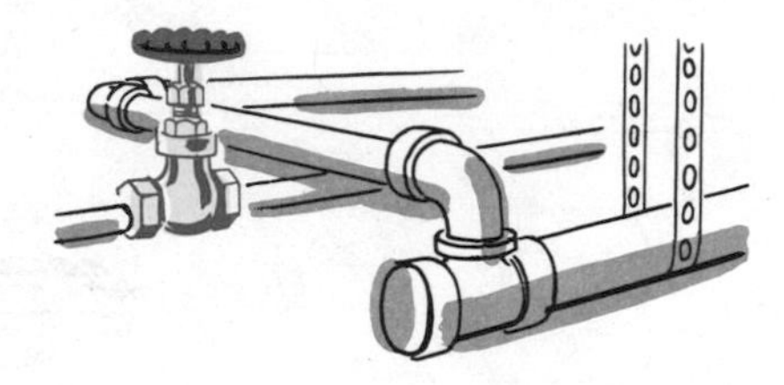

City water comes out of a **pipe**. Gas goes through a pipe. **Pipes** are also used to carry oil all over the United States.

---

pit A **pit** is **a hole in the ground.** Coal mines are pits.

---

pitcher 

We pour from a **pitcher**. A cream pitcher is small. A water pitcher is large.

A baseball **pitcher** throws the ball to the man who is at bat. My father took me to a baseball game. The pitcher threw a fast ball.

place My **place** at the table is where I sit at the table.

My toys are in the toy box. That is the **place** for them. That is where they should be.

I scratched my leg in two **places.**

I scratched my leg in two **spots.**

I have lost my **place** in the book. I can't find where I stopped reading.

New York is a **place** I should like to see.

New York is a **city** I should like to see.

I will **place** my doll in her chair.

I will **put** my doll in her chair.

placed I **placed** the dishes on the table.

---

plain The man spoke in **plain** words.

The man spoke in **simple and easy** words.

My new dress is too **plain.** It does not have enough trimming to make it look pretty.

A **plain** is **smooth and flat country.** In the West, cattle live on the **plains.**

plan

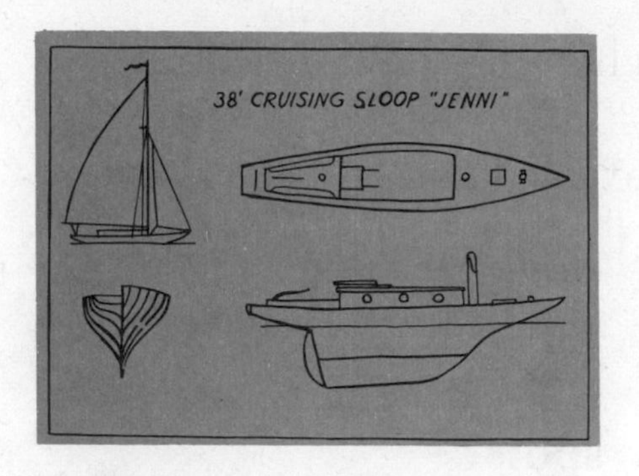

This is a **plan** for a boat. It is a drawing that shows how the boat is to be built.

We **plan** to go.
We **expect** to go.

We will **plan** our trip before we go.
We will **think out** our trip before we go.

---

plane An **airplane** is sometimes called a **plane.** The **planes** fly over our house on their way to the airport.

---

plant A rose bush is a **plant.** Bushes, trees, grass, vegetables, flowers, and weeds are all called **plants.**

See John **plant** the seeds.

See John **put** the seeds **in the ground.**

Factories are sometimes called **plants.**

---

plastic A **plastic** can be made into any shape, or into sheets or film. Many things that used to be made of wood, metal, or cloth are now often made of **plastic.**

plate Mother put my lunch on a **plate.**

Here is a row of pretty **plates.** We have other dishes, too.

---

play John likes to **play** with Rover. They have fun.

Ellen is learning to **play** the violin.

Ellen is learning to **make music** on the violin.

Mary acted in a **play.**

Mary acted in a **show.**

Joe is going to **play** that he is a clown.

Joe is going to **act like** a clown.

I woke before the morning, I was happy all the day,
I never said an ugly word, but smiled and stuck to play.

played We **played** ball in our yard.

playing The cat is **playing** with the ball.

---

player A **player** is **anyone who plays a game.** We need another player for our baseball team.

playground We play on the **playground** at school or in the park. The playground of our school has swings and seesaws in it. We take turns on the slide. Some of the children play in the box of sand.
Bob and I like to wade in the pool in our park. All the children like to come to the playground.

---

playhouse This is Sarah's **playhouse.** A playhouse is like a real house, but much smaller.

playing The cat is **playing** with the ball.
The cat is **having fun** with the ball.

Jack is **playing** that he is a clown.
Jack is **acting like** a clown.

Ellen is **playing** the piano.
Ellen is **making music** on the piano.

playmate Your **playmate** is the **boy or the girl you play with.**

pleasant We spent a **pleasant** evening at the park.
We spent an evening **that pleased us** at the park.

please A gentle, polite child says **please.** Anne says, "May I have some cake, please?"

I will **please** my mother if I am a good child.

It will **make** my mother **feel good** if I am a good child.

---

plenty There is **plenty** of milk.

There is **all** the milk **that is needed.**

---

plow A **plow** is used to cut and turn over the ground so that seeds can be planted.

The farmer will **plow** his land this spring.

plowing We like to watch the farmer when he is **plowing.**

---

plum A **plum** is a fruit. **Plums** grow on a plum tree. There are red plums, blue plums, and yellow plums.

Little Jack Horner sat in a corner,
Eating his Christmas pie;
He put in his thumb, and pulled out
a plum,
And said, "What a good boy am I!"

---

pocket I have a **pocket** in my overalls. I put small things in my pocket.

I have three **pockets** in my coat.

pocketbook A **pocketbook** is a **purse.** Mother keeps money in her pocketbook.

---

poem This is a **poem** by Robert Louis Stevenson.

A birdie with a yellow bill
Hopped upon the window sill,
Cocked his shining eye and said:
"Ain't you 'shamed, you sleepyhead?"

---

point

See Mary **point** at the bird. She **points** with her finger to show where it is.

A needle has a sharp **point.**

A needle has a sharp **end.**

pointed John **pointed** at the boats far out in the lake.

---

poison Anything that is a **poison** will make you very sick if you eat it. Never put poison in your mouth.

---

pole

A telephone **pole.**

These boys are fishing with fishing **poles.**

A flag pole.

policeman

A **policeman** helps me across the street on my way to school. A policeman protects people.

---

policemen Some **policemen** guard the streets. Some policemen ride in cars. Other policemen ride horses.

---

polite James is **polite.**

James is **kind and thoughtful of others.** He says "Please" and "Thank you."

---

pond A **pond** is a **small lake.** Fish swim in the water of a pond. Some plants grow in it.

---

ponies

There are two **ponies** here for children to ride.

---

pony A **pony** is a **small horse.**

I had a little pony,
His name was Dapple Gray;
I lent him to a lady
To ride a mile away.

pool

We swim in the swimming **pool.** The small children wade in the wading pool.

After it rained, there were small **pools** of water in the streets.

---

poor The woman in the story was **poor.** She didn't have good clothes or good food. She didn't have much money.

We feel sorry for Baby when she falls down. We say, "**Poor** Baby."

Mary did **poor** work in school because her eyes hurt.

Mary did **bad** work in school because her eyes hurt.

---

pop **Pop** is a kind of drink. Some pop is red. Some pop is yellow.

The balloon will **pop.**

The balloon will **burst and make a noise.**

---

porch Our **porch** is outside the house. It is like a room outdoors. We sit on the porch in the summer.

---

post

A fence **post.**

A sign post.

postcard When I was away, I wrote to my friend on a **postcard.** I sent the postcard by mail.

---

postman

Here is the **postman.** He is bringing our letters and magazines to our house.

---

pot

A metal **pot** for cooking food.

A pot for baking beans.

A flower pot.

---

potato A **potato** is a vegetable.

---

potatoes

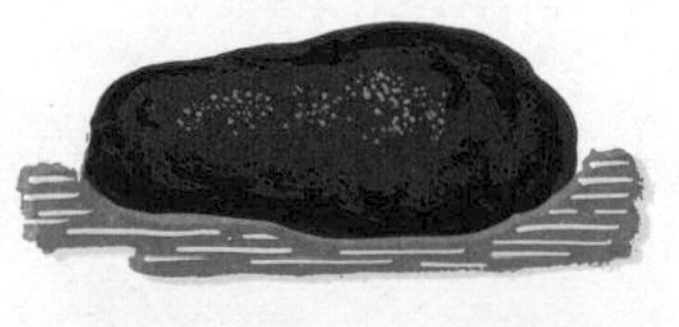

Potatoes are white with a brown skin.

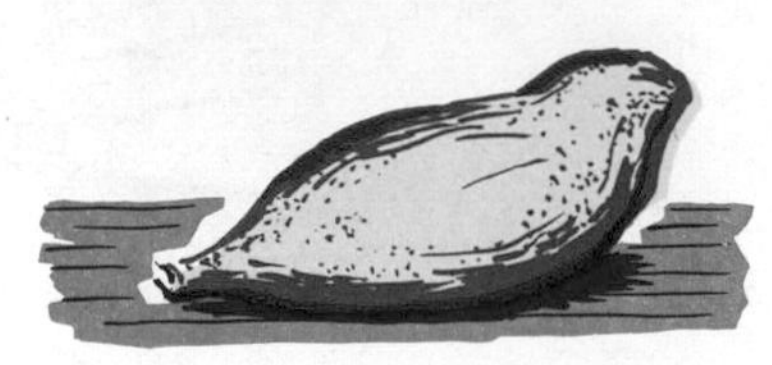

Sweet potatoes are yellow or orange.

Potatoes grow in the ground. We had mashed potatoes for dinner.

pound A **pound** is a measure of weight. My mother went to the store and bought a pound of sugar, a pound of coffee, and a pound of butter.

Jimmy weighs sixty **pounds.**

Father will **pound** the nail with a hammer.

Father will **hit** the nail with a hammer.

pounding He is **pounding** the nail into the wall.

---

pour Joe likes to **pour** water for the elephant. My mother will pour our milk for us. If you turn the tap on, water will pour out.

poured Mary **poured** lemonade into her glass.

---

powder Katherine is putting face **powder** on her face. Flour is a fine powder. We powder the baby to keep him cool after his bath.

---

pray

Now I lay me down to sleep,
I **pray** the Lord my soul to keep.

---

prayer This was the **prayer** Betty said before she went to bed.

present All were **present** except one.

All were **there** except one.

Daddy gave me a set of paints for a Christmas **present.**

Daddy gave me a set of paints for a Christmas **gift.** There were many **presents** under the Christmas tree.

---

president The **President** of our country is chosen by the people.

The **leader** of our country is chosen by the people.

The president of our club is chosen by us.

---

press Elizabeth will **press** her dress.

Elizabeth will **iron** her dress **smooth.**

I **press** the door shut gently.

I **push** the door shut gently.

pressed I **pressed** the lid of the box down.

---

pretend Let's **pretend** I'm a princess and you're a prince.

Let's **make believe** I'm a princess and you're a prince.

---

pretty Baby is **pretty.**

Baby is **nice to look at.**

---

price The **price** of the toy is fifty cents.

The **money it takes to buy** the toy is fifty cents.

prince The son of a king is a **prince**.

princess The daughter of a king is a **princess**.

prize

Ned's dog won a **prize** at the show. He was one of the best dogs there.

The one who runs fastest will win the prize in the race.

promise I **promise** to go.

I **give my word** that I will go.

When I make a promise to my mother I always keep it.

promised I **promised** to take my little sister to the park.

proper Winter is the **proper** season to wear a warm coat.

Winter is the **right** season to wear a warm coat.

It is **proper** to say, "Thank you."

protect My big dog will **protect** me.

My big dog will **take care of** me.

proud My father was **proud of** me when I won the race.

My father was **pleased with** me when I won the race.

---

pudding

We eat **pudding** at supper. Sometimes we have rice pudding. Sometimes we have bread pudding. We have plum pudding for Christmas dinner.

---

puff Sally puts powder on her face with a powder **puff.**

Frank blew the candles out with one **puff.**

Frank blew the candles out with one **quick, hard breath.**

The engine went "**Puff,** puff," as it climbed the hill.

The big bad wolf said to the little pig, "**I'll** huff and **I'll puff** and **I'll** blow your house in."

puffed So he huffed and he **puffed** and he blew the house in.

---

pull When you **pull** something, you try to move it toward you.

Jane likes to pull the sled when Baby rides.

Baby tries to pull my hair.

pulled The horses **pulled** the wagon up the hill.

pumpkin A **pumpkin** is a very large yellow fruit. **Pumpkins** grow on vines. Did you ever eat pumpkin pie? When you make a face in a pumpkin it is called a jack-o'-lantern.

> Peter, Peter, Pumpkin Eater
> Had a wife and couldn't keep her.
> He put her in a pumpkin shell,
> And there he kept her very well.

---

puppies Our dog has three **puppies.**

---

puppy  A **puppy** is a **baby dog.**

---

purple 

Purple is a color.

These flowers are purple. 

---

purse  Mother has a **purse.** She carries money and small things in her purse.

Here are other **purses.**  

push When I sit in my swing, I say, "Give me a **push,** please."

When you **push** something, you try to move it away from you.

See the elephant push the circus wagon.

pushed I **pushed** Bill away so that I could get the ball.

---

pussy Another name for my **kitten** is **pussy.**

I love little pussy, her coat is so warm,
And if I don't hurt her, she'll do me no harm;
I'll not pull her tail, nor drive her away,
But pussy and I very gently will play.

---

put Joan **put** the ball on the table.
Joan **set** the ball on the table.

The boys **put up** a tent.
The boys **set up** a tent.

---

puzzle

My sister got a jigsaw **puzzle** for her birthday. It was a picture cut into many pieces. We fitted the pieces together to make the picture again.

Did you ever tell a riddle? That is a **puzzle** with words.

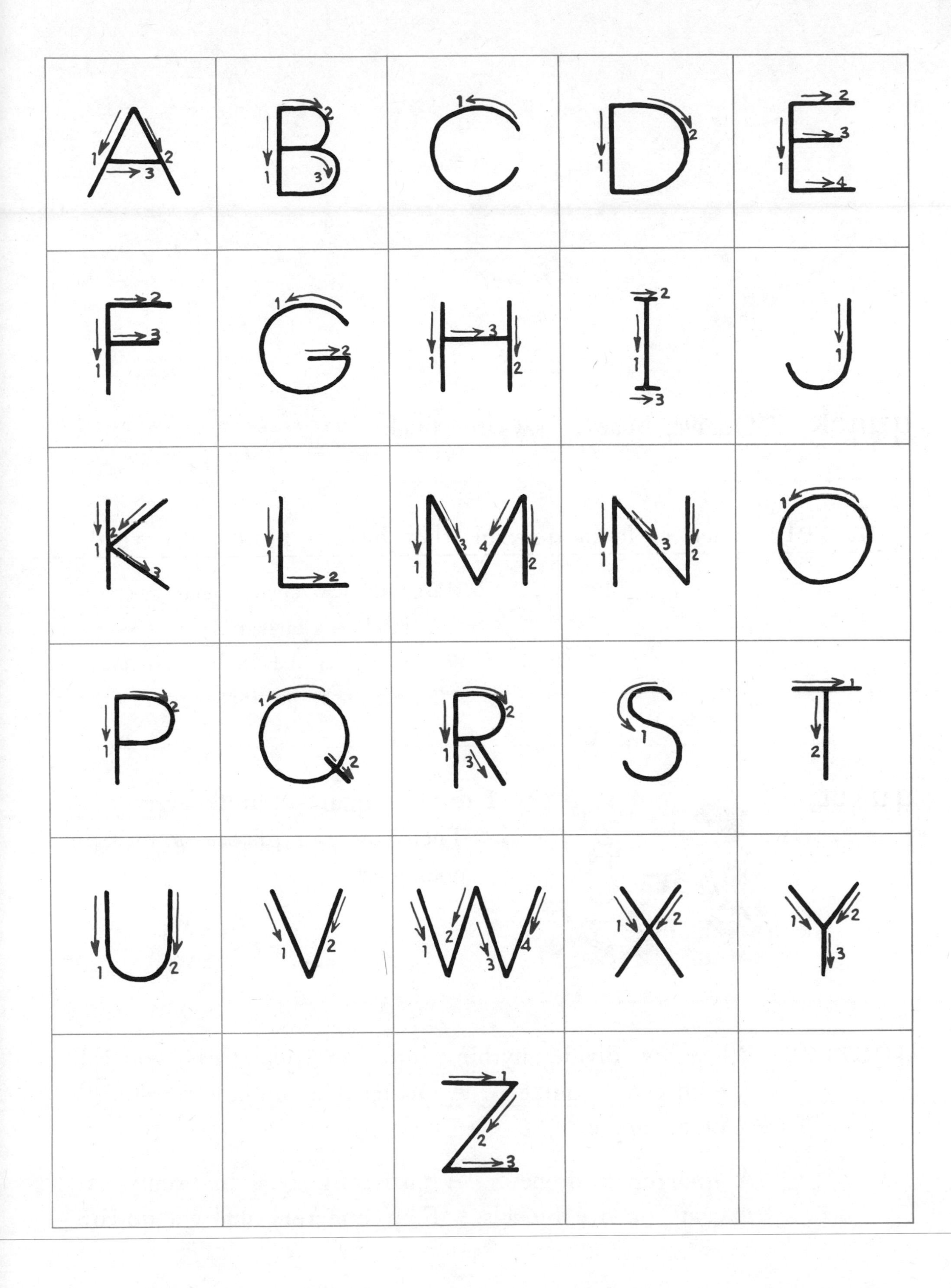
A
B
C
D
E
F
G
H
I
J
K
L
M
N
O
P
Q
R
S
T
U
V
W
X
Y
Z

Q q

quack "**Quack**, quack," says the duck.

quarrel When children **quarrel**, they **have a fight with words.**

"Just then flew down a monstrous crow,
As black as a tar-barrel;
Which frightened both the heroes so,
They quite forgot their quarrel."

quart

I drink a **quart** of milk every day. There are four glasses of milk in one quart.

quarter When you divide anything into four equal parts, you call each part a **quarter.** A quarter of an apple is one-fourth of an apple.

A **quarter** is money. A quarter is equal to twenty-five cents or five nickels. Four **quarters** make a dollar.

queen A **queen** is the head of the people in her country. The wife of a king is also called a queen.

The king was in the counting house
Counting out his money;
The queen was in the parlor
Eating bread and honey.

---

queer

A dragon is a **queer-**looking animal.

A dragon is a **strange-**looking animal.

The cat's paws are **queer.**

The cat's paws are **different from most.** Each paw has six toes.

---

question When I want to find out something, I ask a **question.** I asked my mother a question. I said, "Where is my doll?" My mother answered my question. She said, "You left your doll on the porch."

This is a question mark—?

quick

Kitty is **quick.**

Kitty is **fast.** She will get away from Rover.

---

quiet The children stopped talking and were **quiet.** They made no noise.

The children stopped running and were **quiet.** They did not move.

---

quietly Sue walked downstairs **quietly.**

Sue walked downstairs **without making a noise.**

We sat **quietly.**

We sat **without moving.**

---

quit Bob **quit** playing because he was tired.

Bob **stopped** playing because he was tired.

---

quite I am **quite** happy.

I am **really** happy.

The shoe was **not quite** large enough.

The shoe was **almost** large enough.

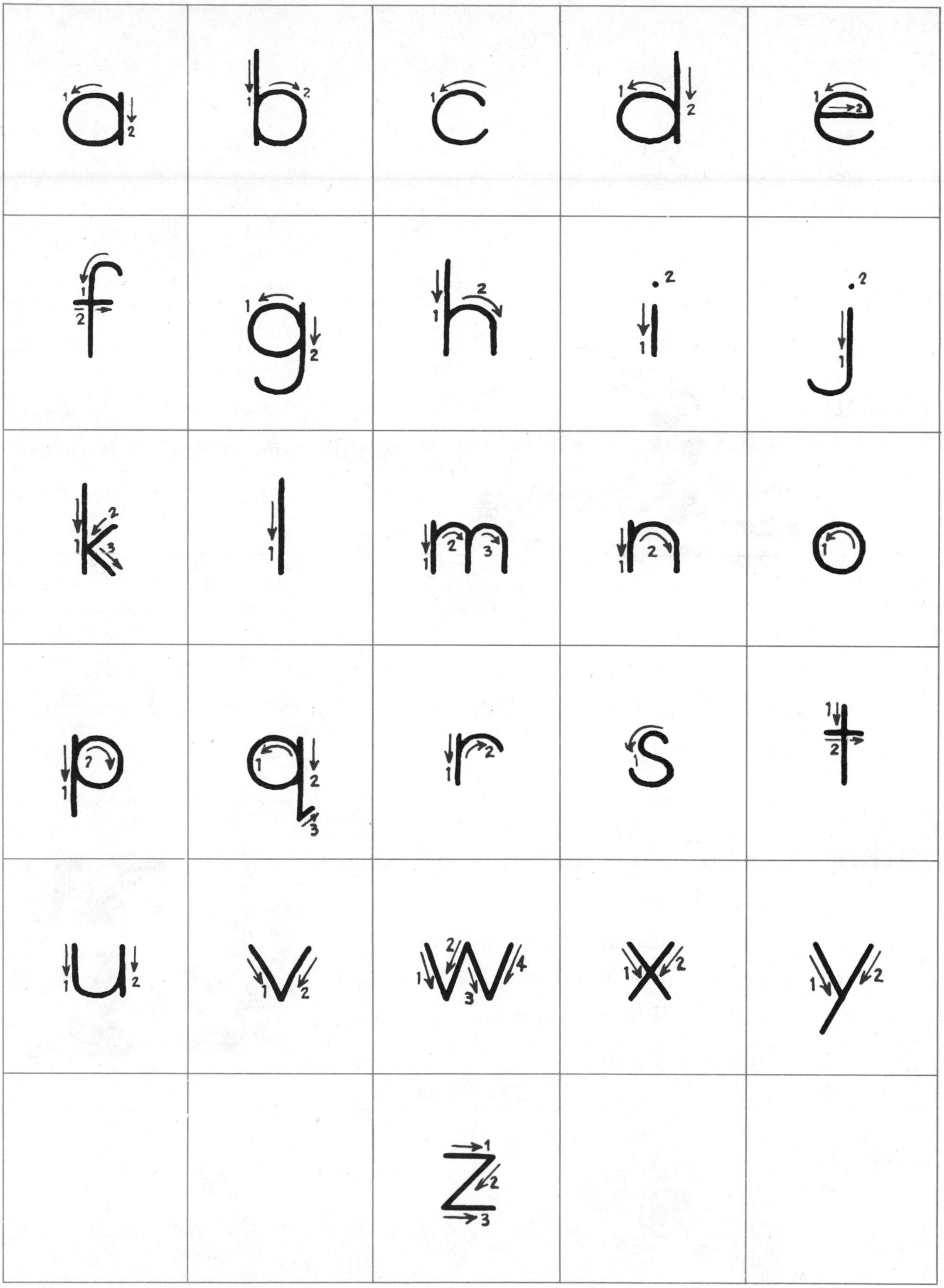

a	b	c	d	e
f	g	h	i	j
k	l	m	n	o
p	q	r	s	t
u	v	w	x	y
		z		

R r

rabbit

A **rabbit** is an animal. It jumps and runs very fast. Two **rabbits** are eating our carrots.

---

race The two boys ran a **race** to the corner. They wanted to see which one would get there first. In a race we find out which person is fastest.

---

radio A **radio.** We hear news and music over the radio. The sound comes through the air without wires. The sound of a telephone comes over wires. That is why a radio is not like a telephone.

---

radish

A **radish** is a vegetable.

The part of the radish that we eat is the root.

radishes We buy **radishes** in a bunch. We grow radishes in our garden. They are good to eat.

---

rag The teacher is cleaning the blackboard with a **rag.**

The teacher is cleaning the blackboard with a **small cloth.**

The scarecrow's clothes were **in rags.**

The scarecrow's clothes were **torn and worn out.**

---

rail There is a **rail** along the stairway at home.

There is a rail on this bridge.

A train runs on **rails.**

A train runs on **bars of iron laid on the ground.**

---

railroad

This is a **railroad** with a train running on it.

This is a **road made of rails** with a train running on it.

---

railway A **railroad** is also called a **railway.**

rain **Water dropping from the clouds** is **rain.**

The sky is full of clouds. Do you think it will **rain?**

rained The ground is wet because it has just **rained.**

raining It is **raining** again. We must hurry inside or we shall get wet.

The rain is raining all around,
It falls on field and tree,
It rains on the umbrellas here,
And on the ships at sea.

---

rainbow A **rainbow** is part of a circle. It has seven colors. You see a rainbow in the sky when the sun shines through the rain.

Dick is looking at the pretty rainbow. It will disappear very soon. A rainbow does not stay in the sky a long time.

---

rained The ground is wet because it has just **rained.**

---

raining It is **raining** again. We must hurry inside or we shall get wet.

raise See Alice **raise** her hand.

See Alice **put up** her hand.

Did you ever **raise** rabbits? My mother won't let me raise rabbits, but I have a kitten.

---

rake

See Bobby **rake** the leaves in the yard.

See Bobby **gather together** the leaves in the yard **with a rake.**

When Bobby will rake another pile of leaves we will jump in it. Bobby knows how to use the rake. He helps his father rake the lawn.

---

ran Peter **ran** down the road.

His dog ran with him.

---

ranch Cattle, horses, or sheep are raised on a **ranch.** Vegetables, grains, or fruits are grown on a farm. Would you rather live on a ranch or a farm?

---

rang The doorbell **rang** a little while ago.

rap

I heard someone **rap** on the door.

I heard someone **hit** on the door.

It was Halloween and Louis wore his clown suit. I went with him to rap on Mike's door. We had fun.

---

rat A **rat** is a small animal. It is like a mouse, but bigger. **Rats** can be brown, black, gray, or white.

This is the rat
That ate the malt
That lay in the house
That Jack built.

---

rather I would **rather** have milk than cocoa. I like it better. I would rather play house than jump rope. It is more fun.

---

raw The apple I ate was **raw.**

The apple I ate was **not cooked.** Some animals eat raw meat. People eat cooked meat.

---

razor Daddy shaves his face with a **razor.**

reach

I can **reach** the apple on this tree.

I can **touch** the apple on this tree **by stretching.**

See Baby **reach** his arms toward Mother.

See Baby **stretch out** his arms toward Mother.

---

read Can you **read** a book?

Can you **look at** a book **and tell what it says?** Mary can. She will read me a story.

When I go to school I will learn how to read. Then Mary will not have to read to me.

reading My class is **reading** a book and learning new words.

---

ready Are we **ready** to go to the picnic? Yes, the lunch is ready and everyone is here.

Now **I am ready** to go to bed.

Now **I feel like** going to bed. I have finished my story.

Peter is always ready on time. He is never late. David is very slow. He is never ready. He will miss the party if he does not get ready.

real The happenings we read in the newspaper are **real.** The happenings we read in a fairy story are not real.

This is my teddy bear.

This is a **real** bear.

---

really I **really** want to be a fireman when I grow up. I'm not fooling you. It's true.

---

reason What is the **reason** for going to town?

Will you **tell me why** we are going to town?

---

receive I will **receive** presents on Christmas.

I will **get** presents on Christmas.

---

recess When work stops, we have a **recess.** Children play at recess.

---

red 

Red is a color.

See Nancy's new red carriage.

reindeer

These are **reindeer.**

A **reindeer** is an animal that can run fast.

The reindeer pull Santa Claus's sled.

---

remain I will **remain** at home until you call for me.

I will **stay** at home until you call for me.

---

remember I will **remember** your name.

I will **keep** your name **in my mind.**

I will **not forget** your name.

---

reply Daddy will **reply to** my letter.

Daddy will **answer** my letter.

---

rest I get a good **rest** when I sleep at night.

I will have to **rest** because I am tired. When we do not work or play, we rest.

Can I eat the **rest** of the cake?

Can I eat the **part that is left** of the cake?

return I will **return** your ball.

I will **give back** your ball.

Anne has gone to see her aunt. She will **return** tomorrow.

She will **come back** tomorrow.

returned I **returned** my book to the library.

---

ribbon

Nancy holds a roll of **ribbon.** Does the ribbon in her hair match her dress?

Betty tied her father's Christmas present with a ribbon.

Oh dear, what can the matter be,
Johnny's so long at the fair.
He promised to bring me a pretty blue ribbon,
To tie up my bonny brown hair.

---

rice **Rice** is a grain. We buy rice at the store. Rice grows in a field. Sometimes we have cooked rice to eat at supper.

---

rich This king is **rich.**

This king **has much money.**

---

ridden The horse was **ridden** until he was tired.

riddle A **riddle** is a **word puzzle.** Can you guess this riddle?

Higher than a house, higher than a tree.
Oh! whatever can that be?

Answer: (A star.)

---

ride You can **ride** in an automobile or a train.
You can ride a bicycle.
You can ride on a horse.

This is the way the ladies ride:
Trot, trot, trot!

This is the way the gentlemen ride:
Gallop-a-trot, gallop-a-trot!

This is the way the farmers ride:
Hobbledehoy! Hobbledehoy!

ridden The horse was **ridden** until he was tired.

riding My big brother is **riding** in an automobile.

rode I **rode** downtown on a bus yesterday.

right Jerry had the **right** answer. Bill had the wrong answer.

It is **right** to tell the truth. It is right to be honest. It is right to be clean and neat.

I am holding up my **right** hand.

That big boy had no **right** to take my ball.

---

ring  This is a **ring**.

Sister got a diamond **ring** for Christmas.

Doesn't it look pretty on her finger?

We stand in a **ring** to play "Drop the Handkerchief."

We stand in a **circle** to play "Drop the Handkerchief."

Listen to the bells **ring.** It is New Year's Eve. I ring the doorbell when I want to get into the house. The telephone bell will ring when someone is calling us.

rang The doorbell **rang** a little while ago.

rung The alarm clock has **rung,** and I must get up.

---

ripe 

We pick fruit when it is **ripe.**

We pick fruit when it is **ready to eat.** One apple is ripe. The other apple is green.

rise What time will the sun **rise?**

What time will the sun **come up?**

I must **rise** from my chair.

I must **get up** from my chair.

The cock doth crow
To let you know,
If you be wise,
'Tis time to rise.

risen The cake in the oven has **risen.**

rose Daddy **rose** when the lady came into the room.

---

river

A **river** is water that runs between two banks. A river is larger than a stream.

On goes the river
And out past the mill,
Away down the valley,
Away down the hill.

---

road We drove along the **road.**

This road goes to Grandfather's house.

roar In winter I like to listen to the **roar** of the wind.

In winter I like to listen to the **loud sound** of the wind.

The lion can **roar.**

The lion can **make a loud noise.**

---

roast

This is a **roast** of meat.

To **roast** meat, you cook it in the oven.

---

rob To **rob** means to **steal** or **take something away from another person.**

---

robber A **robber** stole some money from the bank downtown.

---

robin A **robin** is a pretty bird with a red breast.

Little Robin Redbreast jumped upon a wall,
Pussy Cat jumped after him and almost got a fall;
Little Robin chirped and sang; what did Pussy say?
Pussy said "Mew" and Robin jumped away.

rock

A **rock** is a **big stone.**

These are **rocks.**

Louise likes to **rock** her doll to sleep. She sings "Rock-a-bye, Baby."

---

rode I **rode** downtown on a bus yesterday.

---

roll Katherine likes to **roll** the snowball down the hill.

Katherine likes to **turn** the snowball **over and over** down the hill.

Mother will **roll up** the rug.

Mother will **wrap** the rug **around and around itself.**

Daddy has a **roll** of wire.

I ate a **roll** for breakfast.

rolled John **rolled** himself up in a blanket.

---

roller

Tom likes to skate on **roller** skates. The little wheels turn around and around as he goes along.

roof The **roof** of our house is red.
The **top** of our house is red.

room

My own **room** is my bedroom.
There are six **rooms** in our house.

Is there **room** for me in the car, or is it full?
Is there **place** for me in the car, or is it full?

rooster A **rooster** is a **father chicken.** The rooster has a comb on his head and long tail feathers. He crows early in the morning.

root A **root** is the **part of a plant below the ground.** Some plants have many **roots.**

rope

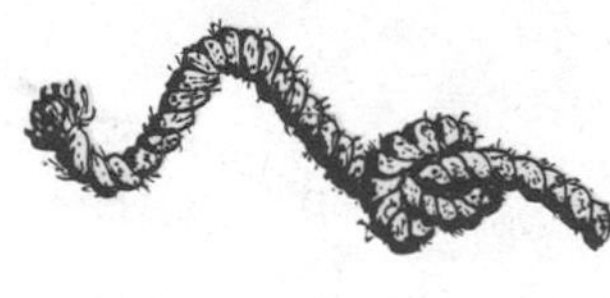

This **rope** has a knot in it.

You can make a swing with rope.
You can jump the rope.

rose

A **rose** is a flower.
Do you like **roses?**

Daddy **rose** when the lady came into the room.
Daddy **got up** when the lady came into the room.

The sun **rose** at seven o'clock this morning.
The sun **came up** at seven o'clock this morning.

---

rosebush Roses grow on a **rosebush.**

---

rough John played with his sister. He was **rough,** and he hurt her.
He was **not gentle,** and he hurt her.

The road was **rough.** There were bumps in it. It was not smooth.

---

round A circle is **round.** A ball is round. Anything shaped like a ball or a circle is round.

---

row Baby put the blocks in a **row.**
Baby put the blocks in a **line.**

The sailor will **row** the boat.

rowed Daddy **rowed** us across the lake in a boat.

rub

Anne will **rub** the window to make it clean.

rubs Mother **rubs** my back when it aches.

---

rubber Joe has lost one **rubber.** He will get his foot wet. He wears his **rubbers** over his shoes. They keep his feet dry.

I put a **rubber** band around my papers. I have rubber heels on my shoes. An auto tire is made of rubber.

---

rude The boy was **rude** to me.

The boy was **not polite** to me.

---

rug

Jane has a **rug** beside her bed. She does not have to step on the bare floor when she gets up. We have a big rug in our front room.

---

rule My mother has made a **rule** that I must be in bed by eight o'clock.

When you play games, you have **rules** to play by. The rules tell you what to do and what not to do.

A king can **rule** the people of his country. They must do as the king wants them to do.

ruler A **ruler** is a **stick for measuring how long** a thing is.

This is a ruler I use in school.

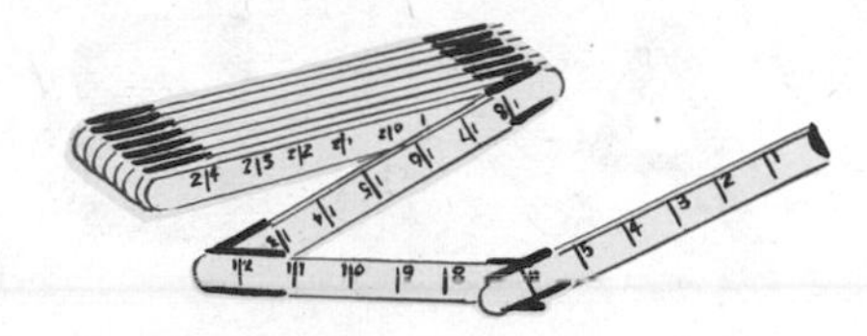

This is a ruler the carpenter uses.

A king is a **ruler.** He rules over his people.

---

run Jane is going to **run** after Peter.

ran Peter **ran** after the dog.

running Jane, Peter, and the dog are all **running.**

---

rung The alarm clock has **rung,** and I must get up.

---

rush Mother said, "I'm in a **rush** to go downtown."

Mother said, "I'm in a **hurry** to go downtown."

We all **rush** out of the house when we hear the fire truck.

We all **go quickly** out of the house when we hear the fire truck.

A	B	C	D	E
F	G	H	I	J
K	L	M	N	O
P	Q	R	S	T
U	V	W	X	Y
		Z		

a	b	c	d	e
f	g	h	i	j
k	l	m	n	o
p	q	r	s	t
u	v	w	x	y
		z		

a	*b*	*c*	*d*	*e*
f	*g*	*h*	*i*	*j*
k	*l*	*m*	*n*	*o*
p	*q*	*r*	*s*	*t*
u	*v*	*w*	*x*	*y*
		z		

S s

sack

A **sack** is a **bag.** Food comes from the grocery in a paper sack. The farmer puts grain in a cloth sack. At the zoo we bought **sacks** of peanuts to feed the elephants.

---

sad I am **sad.**

I am **not happy.**

---

saddle

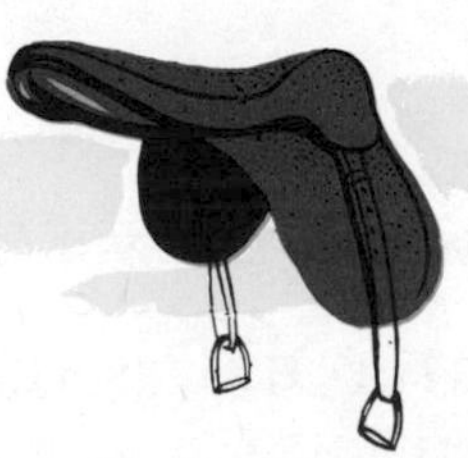

This is a **saddle.**

We put the saddle on the horse's back.
It is a seat for the person who rides the horse.

safe I am **safe** in my own house. Nothing bad can happen to me.

The policeman takes me across the street. I am **safe** from the autos.

I am **not in danger** from the autos.

---

said Dick **said** something I didn't hear.

Dick **spoke** something I didn't hear.

Simple Simon met a pieman,
Going to the fair;
Said Simple Simon to the pieman,
"Let me taste your ware."

Said the pieman to Simple Simon,
"Show me first your penny,"
Said Simple Simon to the pieman,
"Indeed, I have not any."

---

sail

There is a **sail** on this boat. The wind blows against the sail. The boat moves fast when the wind blows hard.

A sailboat will not **sail** unless the wind blows.

A sailboat will not **move on the water** unless the wind blows. But a boat with an engine can sail without wind.

sailing The big ship is **sailing** out to sea.

sailor

This man is a **sailor.** He works on a ship. He lives on the ship when he is working. There are many **sailors** in our Navy.

---

sale We saw a house for **sale.** The people that owned it wanted to sell it.

---

salt I put **salt** on my egg. Food tastes better with salt in it. Sea water has salt in it. Most of the salt we eat comes from under the ground.

---

same My sister and I both have pink dresses. They are the **same.**

They are **just alike.**

Ted and I went to the beach on the bus. We came home the **same** way.

---

sand

Sand is made up of **very tiny pieces of rock.** The sand in our sand pile came from the beach. James is filling a pail with sand.

sandwich

Do you like to eat a **sandwich** for lunch? This is a sandwich made of bread and meat.

---

sandwiches **Sandwiches** are also made with cheese, peanut butter, and other things. We take sandwiches to eat when we have a picnic.

---

sang The children **sang** together.

The children **made music with their voices** together.

---

sank The ship **sank** in the water.

The ship **went down** in the water.

Santa Claus

Santa Claus comes at Christmas
time
To make all children merry.
His beard is white, his smile
is bright,
And his nose is red as a cherry.

In some countries, Santa Claus is called Saint Nicholas.

---

sat Grandfather **sat** down in his chair.

Saturday **Saturday** is the **seventh day of the week.** Children do not go to school on Saturday. Every Saturday Nancy and Joe help their mother with her work.

Sunday Monday Tuesday Wednesday Thursday Friday Saturday

---

saucer  A **saucer** holds a cup for Daddy's coffee.

A saucer holds milk for the kitty.

I put cups and **saucers** on the table.

---

save I **save** part of my money.

I do not spend part of my money. I put it in my bank.

---

saw 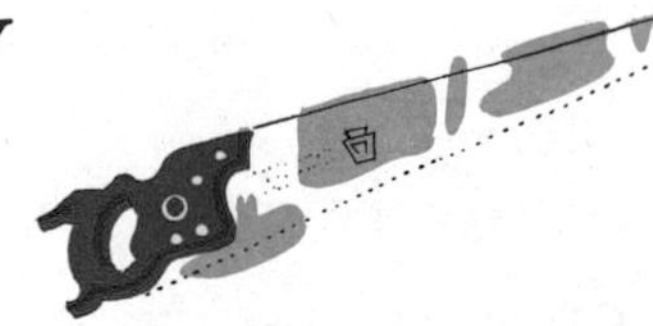 A **saw** cuts wood. The edge of a saw has small, sharp teeth.

Watch Bill **saw** the board.

Watch Bill **cut** the board **with a saw.**

saw We **saw** a parade yesterday.

After my mother explained the story, I **saw** what it meant.
After my mother explained the story, I **knew** what it meant.

We went to the farm and **saw** my aunt.
We went to the farm and **visited** my aunt.

---

say I **say**, "I can't hear you, Dick."

said Dick **said** something I didn't hear.

saying Now he is **saying** it again.

says Dick **says**, "What grade are you in?"

---

scare You cannot **scare** me with your Halloween false face.
You cannot **make** me **afraid** with your Halloween false face.

Mother said, "It gave me a **scare** when you didn't come home."
Mother said, "It gave me a **scared feeling** when you didn't come home."

---

scarecrow

A **scarecrow** is made of sticks and dressed like a man. It is put in the field to scare the crows away.

scared When the tiger growled, I was **scared.**

When the tiger growled, I was **afraid.**

---

school In **school** we learn to read and to write. We draw and paint pictures in school. We go to school early in the morning.

A **school** is a **schoolhouse.**

---

schoolroom Our **schoolroom** has desks and blackboards in it. We learn our lessons in the schoolroom.

---

science When we learn how plants and animals grow, we are learning facts about **science.**

They are called **scientific** facts.

---

scissors

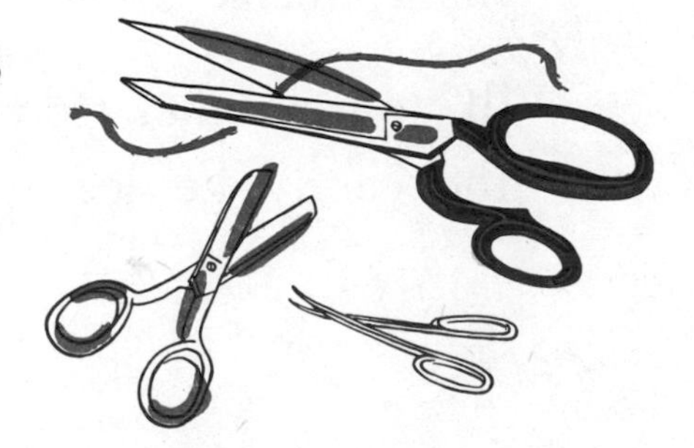

I cut paper with **scissors.** My scissors have round ends. Mother cuts thread and cloth with scissors. Her scissors have sharp points. Mother uses the tiny scissors to trim her fingernails.

scold I do not like to have my sister **scold** me.
I do not like to have my sister **say cross words** to me.

---

scooter I will take a ride on my **scooter.** It has two wheels. I can make my scooter go as fast as my dog runs.

---

scout A Boy **Scout** wears a uniform. A Girl Scout wears a uniform, too. There are Girls **Scouts** and Boy Scouts all over the world. They belong to a big club.

---

scrap Her mother gave Ellen a **scrap** of cloth to make a doll dress.
Her mother gave Ellen a **small piece** of cloth to make a doll dress.

---

scrape

Robert will **scrape** the mud off his rubbers.

Will your mother let you **scrape** the candy kettle?

scratch I have a **scratch** on my knee.
I have a **little cut** on my knee.

The doctor says I must not **scratch** my mosquito bites.
The doctor says I must not **rub** my mosquito bites **with my fingernails.**

Did you see the cat **scratch** my hand with his claws?
Did you see the cat **make little cuts** in my hand with his claws?

See the rooster **scratch** the ground.
He is looking for bugs to eat.

scratched Billy **scratched** himself on a nail.

---

scream I thought I heard a **scream.**
I thought I heard a **loud cry.**

The children **scream** when they are playing.
The children **cry out loudly** when they are playing.

scrub

Cinderella must **scrub** the floor to make it clean.

Cinderella must **wash and rub** the floor to make it clean.

---

sea The **sea** is salt water and covers most of the earth. It is sometimes called the ocean. Ships travel on the sea. Fish swim in the sea.

---

season Summer is a **season.** The four **seasons** of the year are spring, summer, autumn, and winter. Which of the four seasons do you like best?

---

seat

Something to sit on is called a **seat.** A chair is a seat. This picture is of a lawn seat. Our **seats** were in the fourth row at the circus.

---

second

first	**second**	third	fourth	fifth
1st	**2nd**	3rd	4th	5th

Harry is standing on the first step.
Mary is standing on the second.
George is on the third.

second A **second** is a measure of time. It is very short. There are sixty **seconds** in a minute.

---

secret **Something that no one else knows** about is your **secret.** I am keeping Mother's present a secret.

Something that is hidden is **secret.** We have a secret drawer in our desk.

---

see I **see** with my eyes. Do you see Joan hiding behind the chair? I see her.

I don't **see** why Billy is so cross today.

I don't **know** why Billy is so cross today.

Tomorrow I am going to the farm to **see** my aunt.

Tomorrow I am going to the farm to **visit** my aunt.

saw We **saw** a parade yesterday.

seen I have not **seen** my aunt for a long time.

---

seed

Almost every plant grows from a **seed.** These are **seeds** that we plant in the vegetable garden to grow corn, peas and beets. The seeds are covered with earth. We plant flower seeds, too.

seem Does this answer **seem** right to you?

Does this answer **look** right to you?

Feel my face. Does it **seem** hot to you?

Does it **feel** hot to you?

Does this candy **seem** too sweet?

Does this candy **taste** too sweet?

seemed The policeman **seemed** to be a strong man.

seems My mother **seems** to be in a hurry.

---

seesaw

Sally and her brother are playing on the **seesaw.** One end of the seesaw goes up while the other goes down. A seesaw is also called a teeter-totter.

---

sell The man will **sell** you a balloon.

The man will **give** you a balloon **for money.**

selling The man is **selling** balloons.

sold He **sold** me a balloon.

send I will **send** you a box of candy.

I will **have someone bring** you a box of candy.

My mother will **send** me to the store.

My mother will **make** me **go** to the store.

sending Tommy is **sending** a letter to his aunt.

sent The teacher **sent** Alice to another room.

---

sense Tim has good **sense.** He knows the right thing to do.

I have a **sense** of taste. I also have a sense of touch, of hearing, of seeing, and of smelling. These are my five **senses.**

---

sent Did you get the box of candy **I sent** you?

Did you get the box of candy **I had someone bring** you?

The teacher **sent** Alice home from school because she had a cold.

The teacher **made** Alice **go** home from school because she had a cold.

September **September** is the **ninth month of the year.** It has thirty days. It comes in the autumn. We go back to school in September after our summer vacation.

January February March April May June

July August September October November December

servant

Susan is paid to help with
the work in the house.
She is a **servant.**

Margaret is paid to wash
and iron the clothes.
She is a servant, too.

---

serve A good American will **serve** his country.

A good American will **help and work for** his country.

The cook will **serve** the turkey.

The cook will **put** the turkey **on the table.**

---

set Ben got a **set** of blocks for a present.

Jane can **set** the table. She puts the dishes and silver on it.

Let me **set** the chair over here.

Let me **put** the chair over here.

seven

As I was going to St. Ives
I met a man with **seven** wives.
Each wife had seven sacks,
Each sack had seven cats,
Each cat had seven kits.
Kits, cats, sacks, and wives,
How many were going to St.
Ives?

As I was going to St. Ives
I met a man with 7 wives.
Each wife had 7 sacks,
Each sack had 7 cats,
Each cat had 7 kits.
Kits, cats, sacks, and wives,
How many were going to St.
Ives?

(Answer: One)

one	two	three	four	five
1	2	3	4	5

six	**seven**	eight	nine	ten
6	7	8	9	10

several

Here is one fish.

Here are **several** fish.
Here are **some** fish.

Five or six people would be several people. But a hundred people would be many people.

sew We **sew** with a needle and thread. Mary will sew a dress for her doll.

sewed She has **sewed** many dresses for her dolls.

sewing Mary is **sewing** with black thread.

---

shade John is sitting in the **shade** of the tree. Louise is sitting in the sunshine. A cloud covering the sun makes shade. An umbrella will give you shade from the sun.

---

shadow When the light shines, almost everything has a **shadow.** You can see your shadow if you stand in the sun. Trees make lovely **shadows** in the moonlight.

I have a little shadow that goes in and out with me,
And what can be the use of him is more than I can see.
He is very, very like me from the heels up to the head;
And I see him jump before me, when I jump into my bed.

shake Harriet will **shake** the dust from the rug. The wet puppy can shake himself to get dry.

shook My mother **shook** the snow from her fur coat.

---

shall I **shall** be happy when summer comes.

You **shall** not tease my kitten.

---

shape

The **shape** of this box is square.

The shape of this box is round.

---

share The boys picked a pail of berries. Each boy took his **share.**

Each boy took his **part.**

Bob and Marjorie will **share** the candy.

Bob and Marjorie will **each have a part of** the candy.

sharp The butcher has a **sharp** knife. It cuts the meat easily. My mother has sharp scissors. They cut the cloth easily.

Pins and needles have **sharp** points.

---

shave

To **shave** means to **cut off hair with a razor.**

shaving Father is **shaving** his face.

---

she Ellen is my sister. I think **she** is a nice girl.

---

shed

At the side of the barn is a low building. It is a **shed.** The farmer keeps his wood in it. It is a wood shed.

---

sheep A **sheep** is a gentle animal. The body of a sheep is covered with wool. Many sheep together are a flock of **sheep.**

sheet Mother puts a clean **sheet** on my bed. The sheet keeps the blankets from touching me.

May I have a **sheet** of paper?

May I have a **piece** of paper?

---

shelf

The clock is on the top **shelf.** The books are on the lower **shelves.**

---

shell

An egg **shell** is the hard outside of an egg. A nut shell is the hard outside of a nut. Mamma breaks the egg shell before she puts the egg in the cake.

I found a sea **shell** near the water. Here are sea **shells.**

---

shelves The books are on the lower **shelves.** The clock is on the top shelf.

---

shine To **shine** means to **send out light.** The lights of the city shine at night.

shines The sun **shines** in the daytime. The moon shines at night.

shone Our automobile lights **shone** on the road.

---

shiny Bob has **shiny** gold buttons on his sailor coat.

Bob has **bright** gold buttons on his sailor coat.

ship A **ship** sails on the water.

A **very big boat** sails on the water. The **ships** sail on the ocean to all parts of the world.

The anchor heaves, the ship swings free,
The sails swell full. To sea! To sea!

shirt

My father has on a blue **shirt.**

shoe A baby's **shoe** is small. A man's shoe is large. We wear **shoes** on our feet.

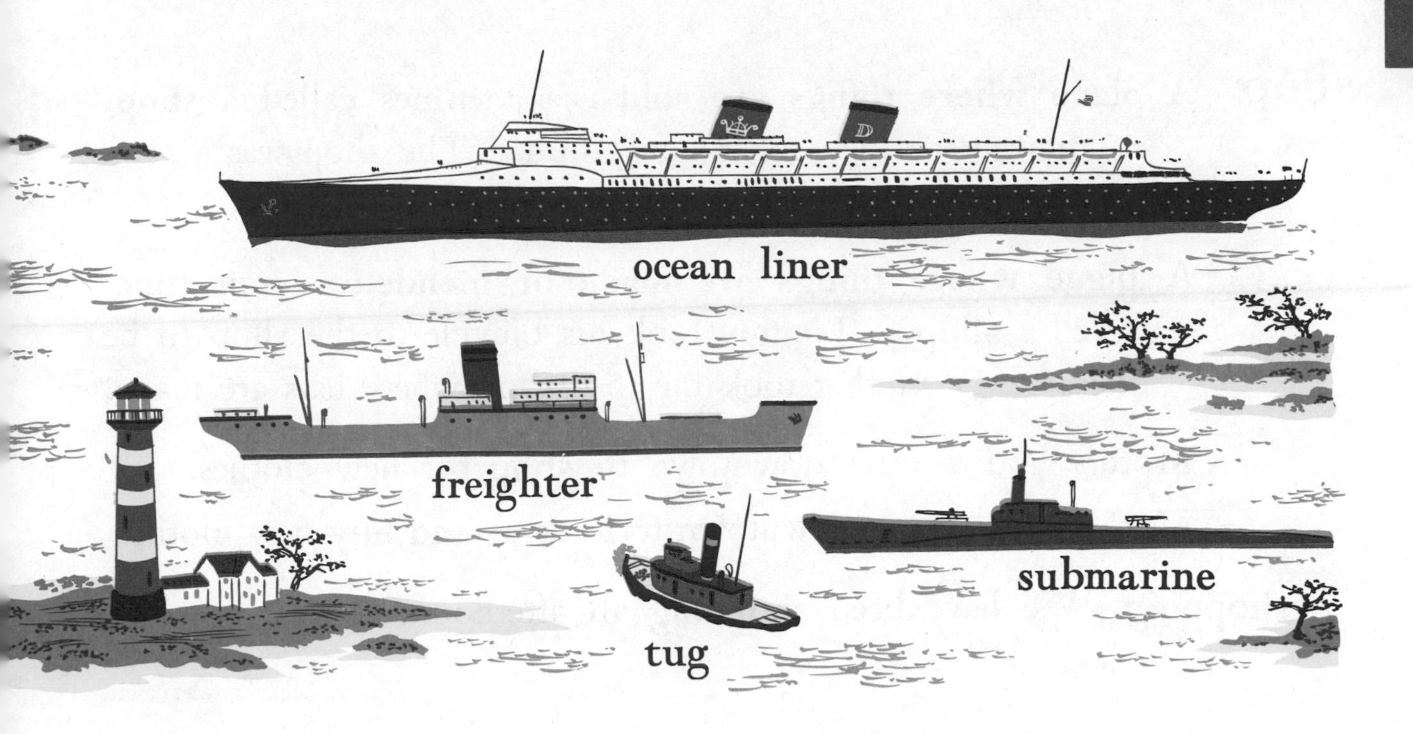

shone Our automobile lights **shone** on the road.

Our automobile lights **sent out light** on the road.

shook My mother **shook** the wet clothes before she hung them on the line.

shoot The men **shoot** at the wild ducks with their guns.

shooting Peter is **shooting** his arrows at the tree.

shot My father **shot** some rabbits on his hunting trip.

shop A **place where things are sold** is sometimes called a **shop.** Susan went to the shop to buy food. The shop was a grocery store.

A **place where things are made or mended** is sometimes called a **shop.** Tommy took his bicycle to the shop to be fixed. My mother took me to a shop where hats are made.

Mother and I went downtown to **shop** for new clothes.

Mother and I went downtown to **look at and buy** new clothes

shopping We have been **shopping** all afternoon.

---

shore The **land at the edge of a body of water** is called the **shore.** We stood on the shore of Lake Erie and looked at the ships on the water.

When I was down beside the sea
A wooden spade they gave to me
To dig the sandy shore.
My holes were empty like a cup,
In every hole the sea came up,
Till it could come no more.

---

short

Bill is **short.** Daddy is tall.

One candle is **short.** Three candles are long.

It will be a **short** time until tomorrow.

---

shot My father **shot** some rabbits on his hunting trip. He shot them with his gun.

should I **should** do as my mother tells me.
I **ought to** do as my mother tells me.

If you **should** see Jack, please give him this book.
If you **happen to** see Jack, please give him this book.

shouldn't **Should not** and **shouldn't** mean the same.
Dan shouldn't tease his sister.

---

shoulder George is carrying a basket on his **shoulder.** Bob climbed up on Jim's **shoulders** to get over the wall.

---

shout The children **shout** when they play games outdoors.
The children **call out loudly** when they play games outdoors.

shouted Larry **shouted** to Roy, "You're it!"

shouting Then everyone started **shouting,** "You're it!"

---

shovel

My sister is clearing the snow from the sidewalk with a snow **shovel.**

Do you like to **shovel** sand into your pail at the shore?

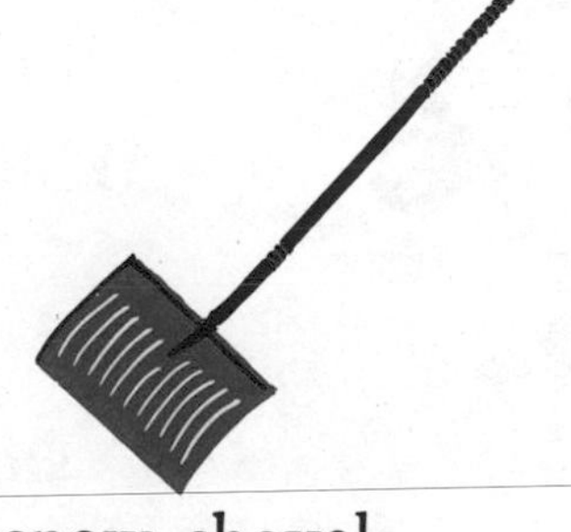

A snow shovel.

A coal shovel.

show We all went to the picture **show.**

Our teacher is going to **show** us a picture of wild animals.

Our teacher is going to **let** us **see** a picture of wild animals.

I will **show** Baby how to walk.

showed Mary **showed** me the new teddy bear she got for Christmas.

---

shower Jerry gave his dog a **shower** of water with the hose.

We got caught in a **shower.**

We got caught in a **light rain.**

I am taking a **shower** bath.

---

shut Please **shut** the window.

Please **close** the window.

---

sick Jack is **sick.**

Jack is **not well.** He has a cold. When Daddy was sick, he went to the hospital.

---

side

One **side** of the clown's suit is red. The other side is yellow.

Which **side** do you want to play on?

Which **group** do you want to play with?

We crossed the street to the other **side.**

sidewalk The **sidewalk** is at the side of the street. People walk on the sidewalk. Automobiles, buses, and trucks run on the street.

---

sight A man must have good **sight** to be in the navy. He must see well.

The airplane went behind the clouds out of **sight.** It could not be seen.

Baby was all dirty. Mother said, "He's a **sight!**"
Mother said, "He's a **thing to see!**"

---

sign

This is the kind of **sign** you see along the road. There is another kind of sign on the corner of our street. It tells the name of the street.

Mother, will you **sign** my paper?
Mother, will you **write your name** on my paper?

---

signal

The policeman gave the **signal** for the children to cross the street. He blew a whistle and waved his arm.

---

silent We were **silent** while Elsie sang. We did not speak.

Falling snow is **silent.**
Falling snow **makes no noise.**

silk **Silk** cloth is made from very soft and fine threads. The silk threads are made by silkworms.

---

silly My kitten is acting **silly.** He is chasing his tail. Sometimes I act silly, too.

Here is a **silly** poem:

Three children sliding on the ice
Upon a summer's day,
As it fell out, they all fell in,
The rest they ran away.

---

silver

These dishes and the spoon are made of **silver.** My knife and fork are made of silver. Some money is made from silver. Silver is a metal.

---

since I have not been to visit Grandmother **since** Christmas.

I have not been to visit Grandmother **from that time until now.**

---

sing

Listen to the children **sing.**

Listen to the children **make music with their voices.**

sang The children **sang** together.

singing They were **singing** "The Star-Spangled Banner."

sung They have **sung** together many times.

singer My brother is a **singer.**

My brother is a **person that sings.**

---

sink Betty is washing dishes in the kitchen **sink.**

I threw a rock in the water and watched it **sink.**

I threw a rock in the water and watched it **go down.**

sank The ship **sank** in the storm at sea.

sunk The soap had **sunk** to the bottom of the bathtub.

---

sir To a man we sometimes say, "Yes, **sir,**" or "No, sir." A soldier says, "Yes, sir," or "No, sir," when he speaks to his captain.

---

sister Joan is Margaret's **sister.** Joan and Margaret have the same father and mother.

---

sit

My dog Chips can **sit** up and ask for food.

sat Grandfather **sat** down in his chair.

sitting Baby is **sitting** on his lap.

---

six 6 This is the figure **six—6.**

One little, two little, three little Indians,
Four little, five little, six little Indians,
Seven little, eight little, nine little Indians,
Ten little Indian boys.

1 little, 2 little, 3 little Indians,
4 little, 5 little, 6 little Indians,
7 little, 8 little, 9 little Indians,
10 little Indian boys.

---

sixty 60 Fifty and ten make **sixty.**

50 + 10 = **60**

ten	twenty	thirty	forty	fifty	**sixty**
10	20	30	40	50	**60**

---

size

Size means **how big** or **how little.**
These two boats are the same size.

---

skate

I will fasten my **skate.**

In winter we **skate** on the ice.

In summer we use roller **skates.**

skating We go **skating** for fun.

skin The covering of your body is your **skin.** When you take a bath, you wash your skin all over.

The covering of animals and plants is the **skin.** You peel the skin from a banana before you eat it.

---

skip Jane can **skip** the rope.

Jane can **jump** the rope

Polly is going to **skip** the second grade. She will pass from the first grade to the third.

---

skirt A girl's **skirt** is the **part of her dress from the waist down.**

Sometimes a skirt is made without a waist. Then the skirt can bc worn with a sweater.

---

sky You can see stars in the **sky** above you at night. You can see the sun in the sky in the daytime. Sometimes there are clouds in the sky.

---

slap Jim was naughty. He gave his puppy a **slap.**

When a mosquito bites me, **I slap** it.

When a mosquito bites me, **I hit** it **with my open hand.**

sled

Paul is playing with his **sled** in the snow.

---

sleep If I don't get enough **sleep,** I feel tired.

Baby has to **sleep** all night and part of the day.

sleeping

When Baby is **sleeping,** he looks like this.

slept He **slept** through all the noise.

---

sleepy James is **sleepy.** He wants to go to sleep.

---

sleeve The **sleeve** of my coat covers my arm.

---

sleigh

A **sleigh** is a **big sled.** Grandfather used to drive a sleigh when there was snow on the roads. Santa Claus has a sleigh pulled by reindeer.

---

slept Baby was so sound asleep that he **slept** through all the noise.

slice I cut off a **slice** of bread. I put jam and butter on it.

Mother will **slice** the cake.

Mother will **cut** the cake **into slices.**

---

slid Yesterday the snow melted and **slid** off the roof.

---

slide There is a **slide** on the playground at school. Jim will go down the slide first then Sally will have a turn.

We **slide** down the haystack in summer. We slide down the snow-covered hill in winter.

---

slip

Be careful not to **slip** on the ice-covered sidewalk.

A girl wears a **slip** under her dress. Betty got a silk slip for a birthday present.

slipped He **slipped** and fell on the ice.

slipper A **slipper** is a **light shoe.** We wear **slippers** in the house.

Jane is putting on her slippers. The shoes she has taken off are also called slippers.

---

slow Bill is **slow.**

Bill is **not fast.** He will be late for school.

---

slowly The wagon moved **slowly** up the hill. It took a long time to go up the hill.

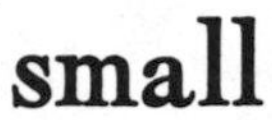

small

The calf is **small.** The cow is large.

The calf is **little.**

smaller The calf is **smaller** than the cow.

smallest The kitten is the **smallest** of these three animals.

---

smell The **smell** of roses is very nice.

I **smell** with my nose.

smelled I **smelled** the cookies that Mother was baking. They smelled good.

smile This man's **smile** shows that he is happy.

When we are happy, we **smile.**

---

smoke As the leaves burned, the **smoke** went up into the sky.

---

smooth My table is **smooth** on top. There are no bumps in it. It is not rough. Glass is smooth, too.

---

snake A **snake** is a long thin animal without legs. A snake moves by crawling.

These are **snakes.** Some snakes might hurt you if you should be too close to them.

snap Mother's purse closes with a **snap.** Have you ever heard the snap of burning wood?

Can you **snap** your fingers?

The dog will **snap** at the cat if she comes near his food.

The dog will **bite quickly** at the cat if she comes near his food.

snapped The turtle **snapped** at the stick.

---

sneeze I am catching cold. **I sneeze.** A sneeze sounds like this: "Kerchoo."

---

snow

Snow is **frozen rain.** I like to see the snow fall, it looks so pretty.

O the snow, the beautiful snow,
Filling the sky and the earth below.
Over the housetops, over the street,
Over the heads of the people you meet,
Dancing,
Flirting,
Skimming along,
Beautiful snow, it can do nothing wrong.

Do you think **it will snow?**
Do you think **snow will fall?**

---

snowball The boy is throwing a **snowball.**

snowflake A **snowflake** is one small piece of snow that falls from the sky.

Some **snowflakes** look like flowers. Some look like stars.

---

snowstorm The snow is falling thick and fast. We are having a **snowstorm.**

---

so It was raining, **so** we wore raincoats.

It was raining; **for that reason** we wore raincoats.

To have your picture taken, hold your head just **so.**

To have your picture taken, hold your head just **this way.**

I have been playing hard and I'm **so** tired.

I have been playing hard and I'm **very** tired.

My mother says, "Is that **so?**"

She means, "Is that **true?**"

I am seven years old, and **so** is Jane.

I am seven years old, and Jane is, **too.**

---

soap I wash my hands with **soap** and water to make them clean.

I use a cake of soap when I wash my hands.

Some people use flakes of soap to wash dishes.

sock

John is putting on his **sock.**
John is putting on his **short stocking.**

Some of his **socks** are white, some are brown, and some are blue.

---

soft A pillow is **soft.** A rock is hard. Kitty's fur is soft to touch.

My mother speaks in a **soft** voice.
My mother speaks in a **low** voice.

---

sold The man **sold** me a balloon.
The man **gave** me a balloon **for money.**

---

soldier

A **soldier** will fight for his country. A soldier is part of the army. The **soldiers** march. They wear uniforms.

---

some Pick out **some** girl to help you.
Pick out **a** girl to help you.

My brother gave me **some** pennies.
My brother gave me **several** pennies.

somebody I heard Mother say that **somebody** is coming to see us.
I heard Mother say that **some person** is coming to see us.

---

someone Is it **someone** we know?
Is it **some person** we know?

---

something There is **something** I cannot see behind that door.
There is **a thing** I cannot see behind that door.

---

sometime I am going to the library **sometime** soon.
I am going to the library **one time or another** soon.

---

sometimes Nancy wears her hair in curls **sometimes.**
Nancy wears her hair in curls **once in a while.**

---

somewhere The sun is shining **somewhere** at all times.
The sun is shining **in some place** at all times.

Are you going **somewhere?**
Are you going **to some place?**

---

son Tommy is Father's **son.** He is also Mother's son. A boy is the son of his mother and father.

song A **song** is made up of **words and music that match.** "The Star-Spangled Banner" is a song.

---

soon Our class at school is going to have a picnic **soon.**

Our class at school is going to have a picnic **in a short time.**

---

sorry

I was **sorry** when my dog hurt his paw. I felt bad.

I am **sorry** I did wrong. I wish I had been good.

I am **sorry** I cannot come to the party. I would like to go.

---

sound A train whistle makes a loud **sound.**

A train whistle makes a loud **noise.** A clock ticking makes little sound. We hear **sounds** with our ears.

Baby fell down, but Mother said he was safe and **sound.**

Baby fell down, but Mother said he was safe and **not hurt.**

---

soup Mother made some **soup** by boiling meat and vegetables in water.

Beautiful Soup, so rich and green,
Waiting in a hot tureen!
Who for such dainties would not stoop?
Soup of the evening, beautiful Soup!

sour Lemon juice tastes **sour.** We put sugar with it to make it sweet.
The milk turned **sour** because it was not kept cold.

---

south As you face the early morning sun, to your right is **south.**
On a map, south is at the bottom.

---

spade

The farmer is digging with a **spade.**
A spade is a kind of shovel.

---

sparrow This bird is a **sparrow.**

---

speak My cat cannot **speak,** but he makes a noise.
My cat cannot **say words,** but he makes a noise.

Look before you leap,
And think before you speak.

spoke Yesterday I **spoke** to my father over the telephone.

spoken My mother has **spoken** to me about keeping my bedroom neat.

speed The horses ran at full **speed.** They ran as fast as they could.

The electric fan has three **speeds:** slow, medium, and fast.

To **speed** means to **go fast.**

speeding The man was stopped for **speeding** in his car.

---

spell I can **spell** my name.

I can **say the letters** of my name **in the right order.**

---

spend I will **spend** twenty cents for candy.

I will **pay** twenty cents for candy.

spent I **spent** sixty cents for a box of crayons last week.

---

spider A **spider** is a bug with eight legs.
It spins a pretty web.

"Will you walk into my parlor?" said
a spider to a fly,
"'Tis the prettiest little parlor that ever
you did spy."

spill Be careful not to **spill** the water on the floor.

Be careful not to **let** the water **fall out** on the floor.

---

spin The top will **spin** when I pull the string.

The top will **turn around and around** when I pull the string.

---

splash Little Billy likes to **splash** in the bathtub.

Little Billy likes to **throw the water about** in the bathtub.

splashed

When Joe threw the stone in the lake, it **splashed.**

---

spoil If you spill ink on your dress, you will **spoil** it. If you boil the candy too long, you will spoil it.

spoiled I dropped my book in the mud and **spoiled** it.

Mrs. Smith said, "Dick is a **spoiled** child."

Mrs. Smith said, "Dick is a **naughty** child **because he has been allowed to do everything he wants to."**

spoke Yesterday I **spoke** to my father over the telephone.
Yesterday I **talked** to my father over the telephone.

---

spoken My mother has **spoken** to me about keeping my room neat.
My mother has **talked** to me about keeping my room neat.

---

spoon I eat soup with a **spoon.**

Here are different kinds of **spoons.**

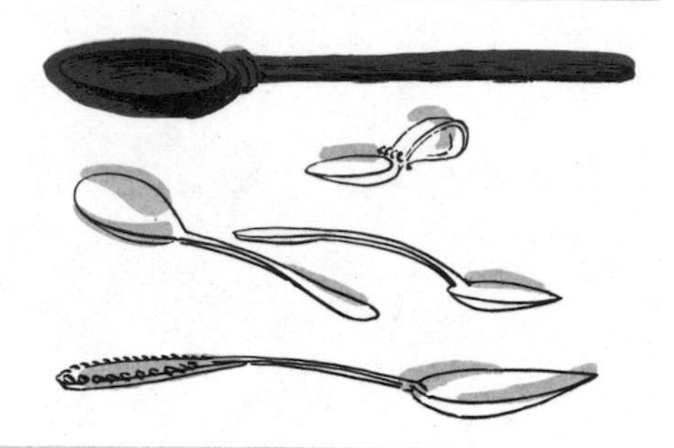

---

spot Sally got a **spot** on her dress. The spot is dirt.

Paul made a **spot** on the paper with ink.
Paul made a **mark** on the paper with ink.

Is this the **spot** where the accident happened?
Is this the **place** where the accident happened?

This dog has many **spots.**

---

spread The dress is **spread** out to dry.
The dress is **opened** out **flat** to dry.

Our sandwiches were **spread** with jelly and peanut butter.
Our sandwiches were **covered** with jelly and peanut butter.

spring **Spring** is **one of the four seasons** of the year. The others are summer, autumn, and winter.

Buttercups and daisies—
Oh, the pretty flowers!
Coming ere the Springtime,
To tell of sunny hours.
When the trees are leafless;
When the fields are bare;
Buttercups and daisies
Spring up here and there.

Spring up means **jump up.**

There are **springs** in my bed that make it easy to lie on.

---

sprinkle When it rains lightly, we say, "It's only a **sprinkle.**"

I like to **sprinkle** the lawn. I sprinkle water on my doll clothes before I iron them. I sprinkle bread crumbs on the snow for the birds to eat.

---

square Nancy is drawing a **square** on the blackboard. A square has four sides. All sides of a square are the same.

squeeze We **squeeze** oranges to get the juice out of them.

We **press** oranges **hard** to get the juice out of them.

Sometimes when you say **squeeze** you mean **hug.** I put my arms around Mother and squeeze her.

squeezed I **squeezed** the suitcase shut.

---

squirrel

A **squirrel** is a small animal with a big, furry tail. A squirrel lives in the trees. He likes to eat nuts.

---

stable I keep my pony in a **stable.** He is fed in the stable. He sleeps in the stable.

---

stair A **stair** is **one step in a group of steps.** All of the steps are the **stairs.** The baby can climb up the stairs.

---

stamp

We put a **stamp** on a letter.

This package has three **stamps** on it. This is the way we pay for having the letter or the package taken where we want it to go.

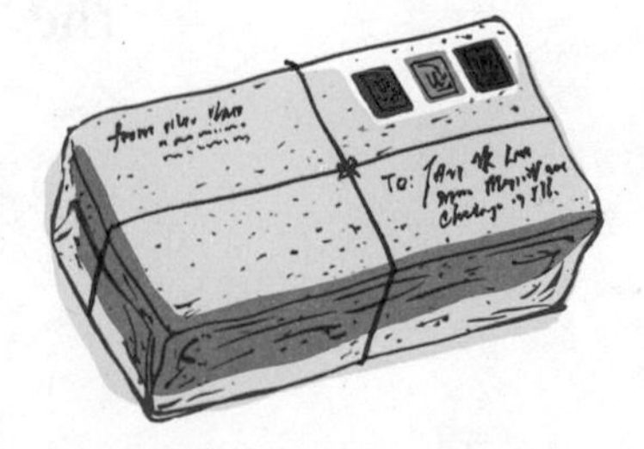

To **stamp** means to **put your foot down hard.**

stamped Jane **stamped** her feet to get the snow off.

stand Let Mary **stand.** Baby will sit down.

Let Mary **be on her feet.** Baby will sit down.

standing Mary is **standing** up. Baby is sitting down.

stood Mary **stood** until Bill brought her a chair.

---

star A **star** makes a bright little light in the sky at night. Many **stars** are in the sky on a clear night. They are really suns. They look small because they are very far away.

There ne'er were such thousands of
leaves on a tree,
Nor of people in church or the
park,
As the crowds of the stars that looked
down upon me,
And that glittered and winked in
the dark.

There are fifty **stars** in the American flag. There is one for each of the fifty states of the United States.

start The parade will **start** from the circus tent.

The parade will **begin to move** from the circus tent.

The ball game will **start** at three o'clock.

The ball game will **begin** at three o'clock.

started The show **started** with music.

---

state We live in the **state** of Ohio. Uncle Jim lives in the state of Texas. What state do you live in? There are fifty **states** in the United States of America.

---

station The big bus stopped at the bus **station.** The train came into the railroad station.

We buy gasoline for our car at a gas **station.**

---

stay I can **stay** here only one hour.

I can **be** here only one hour.

stayed Have you ever **stayed** away from home over night?

steal If you **steal,** you **take something that is not yours.** The dog is going to steal a bone.

stole

Tom, Tom the piper's son,
Stole a pig and away he run.

---

steam When water gets very hot, it boils and becomes **steam.** Watch the steam come out of the tea kettle. Some engines are run by steam. They are steam engines.

---

steep There is a **steep** hill near our house. The path on it goes almost straight up.

---

step When we walk, we take one **step** after another. Baby is taking his first step. He is learning to walk.

When he goes up and down stairs, he puts both feet on each **step.**

I am trying to be quiet, so **I step** lightly.

I am trying to be quiet, so **I walk** lightly.

Jane and her brother are walking up the **steps.**

stepped Robert **stepped** around the mudhole.

stick A **long, thin piece of wood** is a **stick.**

Don't **stick** my hand with the pin.

Don't **put the sharp point** of the pin **in** my hand.

You should **stick** the stamp on the letter.

You should **fasten** the stamp on the letter.

stuck The car got **stuck** in the mud.

---

stiff My new shoes feel **stiff.** They do not bend easily when I walk.

---

still The dog had been barking. Then he became **still.** He didn't make any noise.

He curled up and lay **still.**

He curled up and lay **without moving.**

The dog **still** hasn't moved.

The dog hasn't moved **up to now.**

---

sting Did a bee ever **sting** you? It feels as though you are being stuck with a pin.

stung Martha was **stung** on the arm by a bee. Her arm hurt and swelled up.

---

stir

Jane can **stir** the soup.

Jane can **move** the soup **round and round with her spoon.**

stocking I hung my **stocking** near the chimney on Christmas eve.

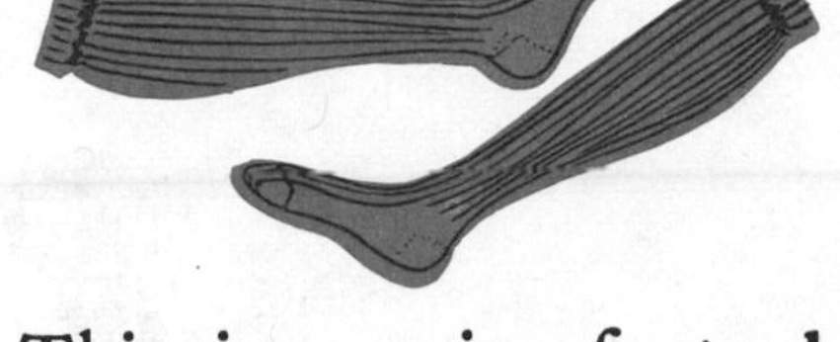

This is a pair of **stockings.**

Diddle, diddle dumpling, my son John,
He went to bed with his breeches on;
One stocking off, and one stocking on,
Diddle, diddle dumpling, my son John.

---

stole The robber was put in jail because he **stole.**

The robber was put in jail because he **took things that did not belong to him.**

Tom, Tom, the piper's son,
Stole a pig and away he run.
The pig was eat, and Tom was beat,
And Tom went roaring down the street.

---

stomach When you swallow food, it goes down your throat and into your **stomach.** Your stomach is a part of your body.

stone A **stone** is a piece of rock. See Bill toss the stone into the air.

My mother's ring has a **stone** in it. The stone is a diamond.

---

stood Mary **stood** until Bill brought her a chair.

Mary **stayed on her feet** until Bill brought her a chair.

---

stool A kind of chair without a back is a **stool.** We use it in the kitchen to sit on. The farmer uses a stool to sit on while he milks the cows.

stop The red light on the street means **"Stop!"**
The red light on the street means **"Do not go any farther."**

"Please **stop** shouting," Mother said. "Don't do it any more."

You can **stop** your ears by putting your fingers in them.

stopped I **stopped** my dog from following me down the street.

stopping The light is red, so the cars are **stopping.**

---

store A **place where things are sold** is a **store.** We buy our food in a grocery store.

The farmer will **store** the corn for his cattle to eat during the winter.

The farmer will **put away** the corn for his cattle to eat during the winter.

When summer comes, my mother will **store** my winter clothes in the attic.

---

storm

The wind blows hard, and the rain pours down. We are having a **storm.** Sometimes thunder and lightning come with a storm.

The snow is falling thick and fast. It is a snow **storm.**

story Aunt Ella is telling a **story.** The story is "The Three Bears."

---

stove This is our kitchen **stove.**

In some houses there is a **stove** to warm the rooms.

---

straight Mary is drawing a crooked line.
Johnny is drawing a **straight** line.

---

strange I will start tomorrow at a **strange** school. I have never been there before.

I will be in a class with **strange** children. I don't know any of them.

A dragon is a **strange**-looking animal.

A dragon is a **queer**-looking animal.

straw

Wheat grains are taken from the wheat plant. The part that is left is **straw.** Straw also comes from other grains. Some straw is used to make straw hats. The pony has straw for his bed.

Sometimes I drink through a paper **straw.**

---

stream A **little river** is a **stream.** The water is not very deep in the stream that runs by our house.

Smooth it slides upon its travel
Here a wimple, there a gleam—
O the clean gravel!
O the smooth stream!

---

street A **street** is a **road in the city or town.** The street I live on is called Main Street. What is the name of your street? There are many **streets** in our town.

---

strength You have to **have strength** to play baseball.

You have to **be strong** to play baseball.

Mary and Bob both have strength. They play baseball. Bob is hitting the baseball. He is strong.

stretch

Tom can **stretch** as high as the top shelf.

Tom can **reach out his arms** as high as the top shelf.

I **stretch** the rubber band.

I **pull out** the rubber band **so that it is longer.**

stretched Bill **stretched** to catch the ball.

---

strike Jerry can **strike** the nail.

Jerry can **hit** the nail.

struck Johnny **struck** the ball with the bat.

---

string We use **string** to tie packages. When you buy string in the store, it is rolled into a ball.

---

strip My belt is made of a **strip** of leather.

My belt is made of a **narrow piece** of leather.

Dick will **strip** and jump into the water.

Dick will **take off his clothes** and jump into the water.

strong

This man is **strong.** He can lift heavy things. He is not weak.

When I read, I like a **strong** light so that I can see well.

Our big swing hangs from a **strong** rope.

Some kinds of cheese have a **strong** taste.

---

struck Johnny **struck** the ball with the bat.

Johnny **hit** the ball with the bat.

---

stuck The car got **stuck** in the mud.

The car got **fastened** in the mud.

Mother **stuck** the needle into the cloth as she sewed.

---

stuff Daddy said, "I don't need the **stuff** in that box."

Daddy said, "I don't need the **things** in that box."

When I make my bear, I will **stuff** it with cotton.

When I make my bear, I will **fill** it with cotton.

stuffed My bed pillow is **stuffed** with feathers.

such I have read several **such** books.

I have read several books **of that kind.**

He was **such** a big dog!

He was a **very** big dog!

---

sugar **Sugar** is made from a plant called sugar cane. It is also made from sugar beets. I sweeten my lemonade with sugar. There is sugar in candy. Sugar makes the candy sweet.

---

suit Bob has on a new **suit.** His suit has a coat and trousers.

Sue is wearing a green **suit.** Her suit has a coat and skirt.

This hat will **suit** me.

This hat will **look good on** me.

I want to do my work so it will **suit** my teacher.

I want to do my work so it will **please** my teacher.

---

summer The **summer** is **one of the four seasons** of the year. The other seasons are autumn, winter, and spring. There is much sunshine in summer. The sunshine makes summer a warm season.

sun

The **sun** shines in the daytime. It is bright and makes you warm.

Great is the sun, and wide he goes
Through empty heaven without repose;
And in the blue and glowing days
More thick than rain he showers his rays.

Sunday **Sunday** is **the first day of the week.** Most people do not go to work on Sunday. Sunday is a day of rest. Many people go to church on Sunday.

Sunday Monday Tuesday Wednesday Thursday Friday Saturday

---

sung The children have **sung** together many times.

The children have **made music with their voices** together many times.

---

sunk The soap had **sunk** to the bottom of the bathtub.

The soap had **gone down** to the bottom of the bathtub.

---

sunshine The **light of the sun** is **sunshine.** Plants grow in the sunshine.

The sunshine is good for children.

---

supper Our **supper** is our **evening meal.**

---

suppose I **suppose** we should go.

I **think perhaps** we should go.

sure I am **sure** that I am eight years old. I am sure that I am a boy.

I am sure that my name is Richard Jones. I know all these things.

---

surprise

We will have a **surprise** party for Joan.

Be quiet so that we can **surprise** Sue.

surprised She will look **surprised.**

---

swallow I **swallow** my food. When food goes down my throat, I swallow it.

---

swam James **swam** to the other side of the pool. He swam by moving his arms and legs in the water.

---

sweater I wear my **sweater** to keep me warm. A sweater is a short jacket made of yarn.

sweep

I **sweep** the floor.

I **brush** the floor **with a broom.** I sweep the floor to clean it.

sweeping Alice was **sweeping** the leaves from the walk.

swept She has **swept** the walk clean.

---

sweet Sugar is **sweet.** Anything made with sugar is sweet. Candy is sweet. Honey is sweet, too.

Mother says, "Baby is so **sweet!**"

Roses are red,
Violets are blue;
Sugar is sweet,
And so are you.

---

swell To **swell** means to **grow bigger.** When I blow air into the balloon, it will swell. George pinched his finger in the door, and it began to swell.

Sometimes the children say, "That's **swell!**"

They mean, "That's **very good.**"

swift The word **swift** means **very fast.** My mother's fingers are swift as she sews. I saw a swift airplane.

---

swim You walk on land and you **swim** in water. Fish are born knowing how to swim. People have to learn to swim. They swim by moving their arms and legs in the water.

Swan, swan, over the sea;
Swim, swan, swim!
Swan, swan, back again;
Well swum, swan!

swam James **swam** to the other side of the pool.

swimming He was **swimming** as fast as his arms and legs could make him go.

---

swing Elsie is in a **swing.** She moves back and forth through the air.

How do you like to go up in a swing,
Up in the air so blue?
Oh, I do think it the pleasantest thing
Ever a child can do!

The monkey can **swing** by his tail.

swinging He is **swinging** from the branch of the tree.

swum James is a good swimmer because he has **swum** so much.

---

swung I **swung** my arms as I walked.

1	2	3
4	5	6
7	8	9
	10	

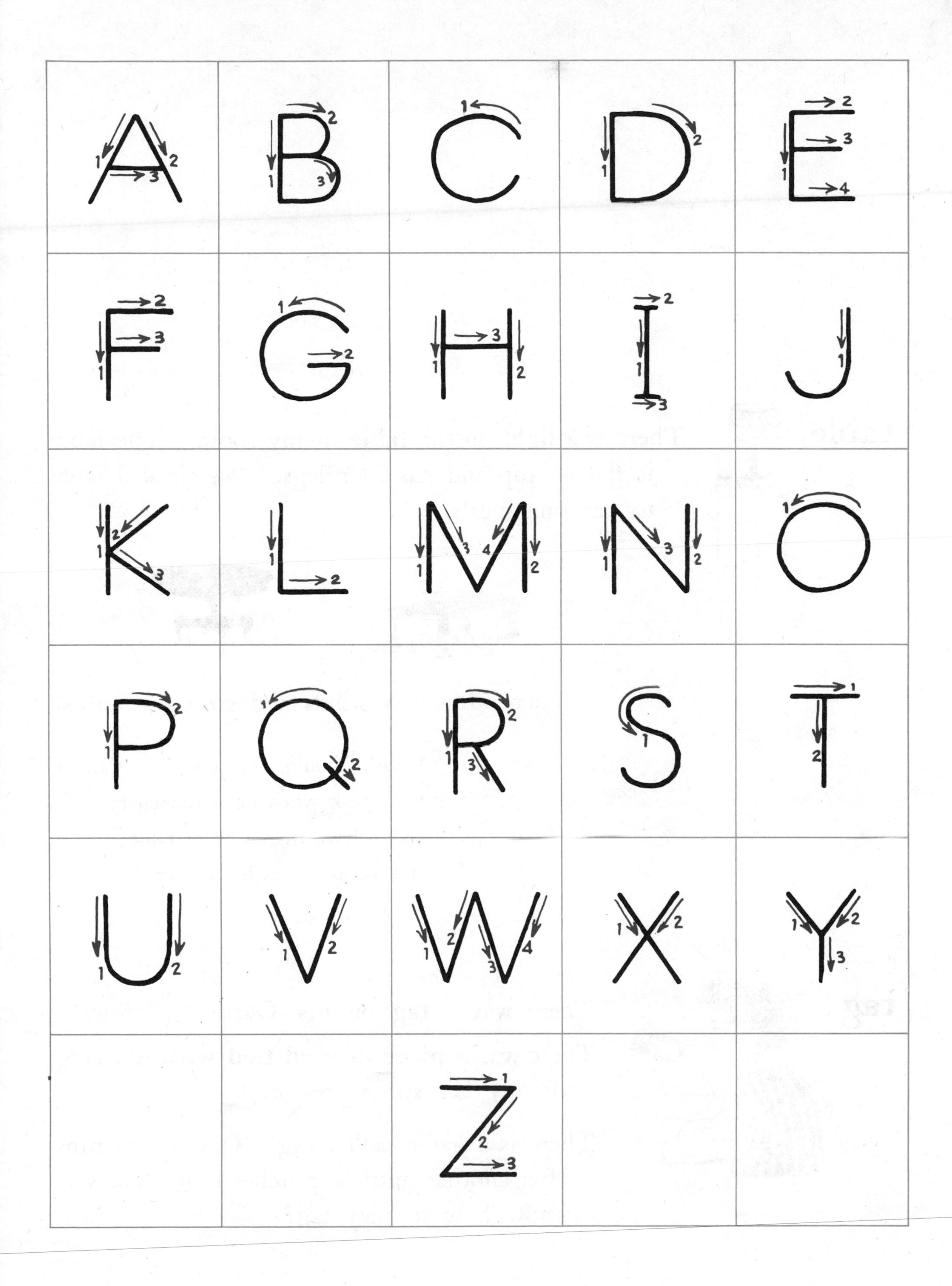

A
B
C
D
E
F
G
H
I
J
K
L
M
N
O
P
Q
R
S
T
U
V
W
X
Y
Z

T t

table 

There is a light on the **table** in my room. The table is flat on top and has four legs. We sit at a table to eat our meals.

There are many kinds and sizes of **tables.**

A child should always say what's true
And speak when he is spoken to,
And behave mannerly at table;
At least as far as he is able.

---

tag 

There was a **tag** on my Christmas present.

There was a **piece of card tied with a string** on my Christmas present.

There is a game called **tag.** One player runs after another until he touches him. Do you know how to play tag?

tail

Does your cat have a **tail?** Does your dog have a tail? A monkey has a tail. A rooster has a tail.

---

take I **take** Mother's hand when we cross the street.

I **get hold of** Mother's hand when we cross the street.

Daddy will **take** us to the ball game.

Daddy will **go with** us to the ball game.

I will **take** a book from the shelf.

I will **get** a book from the shelf.

I will **take** five minutes to get ready.

I will **need** five minutes to get ready.

We **take** a bus to go downtown.

We **ride on** a bus to go downtown.

You **take** the stairs to the second floor.

You **walk on** the stairs to the second floor.

Take this package to Mother.

Carry this package to Mother.

taken George has **taken** one cookie.

takes Mother **takes** me to the show.

taking Jerry is **taking** a ride on his sled.

took Anne **took** her books home with her.

tale Our kindergarten teacher told us the **tale** of "Little Red Riding Hood."

Our kindergarten teacher told us the **story** of "Little Red Riding Hood."

---

talk

To **talk** means to **say words.** I can talk to my dog, but my dog cannot talk to me.

talked I **talked** to Jack over the telephone.

talking I was **talking** about the animals I saw at the circus.

---

tall Daddy is **tall.** I am short.

---

taller I am **taller** than my little sister, but Daddy is taller than I am.

---

tallest Daddy is the **tallest** person in our family.

---

tame A **tame** animal is one that is not afraid of people. Dogs and cats and horses are tame animals. Lions and tigers are wild animals.

---

tan Paul wore **tan** shoes.

Paul wore **light brown** shoes.

Fred played in the sun every day. He got a nice **tan.**

tank A **tank** is a big machine with guns on it. It is used to fight wars.

A tank does not need a road to travel on. It can ride over rough ground.

We put gasoline in the **tank** of our car.

A hot water **tank** holds water to be heated for baths.

---

tap We heard a **tap** on the window.

We heard a **light knock** on the window.

Will you **tap** that boy on the shoulder?

Will you **touch** that boy on the shoulder?

tapped Did you ever play "Tap the Icebox"? In that game the child who is "it" must guess who **tapped** his back.

---

tardy I must not be **tardy** to school.

I must not be **late** to school.

---

taste Sugar has a sweet **taste.** Lemons have a sour taste.

Baby likes to **taste** any new food before she eats it.

Baby likes to **take a little bite of** any new food before she eats it.

tasted I **tasted** the cake. It tasted good.

taught

Larry **taught** his dog to do tricks. Larry **helped** his dog **learn** to do tricks.

---

tea Mother sometimes drinks **tea.** She makes it by putting leaves of a tea plant in hot water.

---

teach Mary's big brother will **teach** her to write her name. Mary's big brother will **help** her **learn** to write her name.

taught I **taught** my dog to run after a stick.

---

teacher My **teacher** at school helps me learn to read. My mother is my teacher in the kitchen. She shows me how to cook.

---

team Several people play together as a **team.** A football team is made up of eleven players. A baseball team is made up of nine players. A basketball team is made up of five players.

Two horses pulling something together are called a **team.**

tear I'm going to **tear** the paper into two pieces.
I'm going to **pull** the paper **apart** into two pieces.

tore I **tore** the paper off the package.

Harry climbed the fence.
He **tore** his pants on the nail.
He **made a hole by pulling** his pants on the nail.

torn Betty's skirt is **torn** where she caught it in the car door.

---

tear A **tear** is a **drop of water that comes from your eye when you cry.** When Tom hurt me, I cried. **Tears** ran down my face.

The tear down childhood's cheek that flows
Is like the dewdrop on the rose.

---

tease We **tease** Sally about the little boy who walks home with her.
We **joke with** Sally about the little boy who walks home with her.

I **tease** my mother to let me go to the circus.
I **ask** my mother **again and again** to let me go to the circus.

Don't **tease** the kitten. He doesn't like it.

teddy bear

My **teddy bear** sits with me at lunch.

---

teeth I chew my food with my **teeth.** My teeth are white and clean. I brush them every day. Each of my teeth is called a tooth.

---

telephone

A **telephone** takes my voice to someone who is far away. My voice goes over the telephone wire. When I was in Chicago, I talked to my mother in Boston by using a telephone.

---

television

We see moving pictures on our **television** set. The pictures show us things that are happening far away. Sometimes television is called TV.

---

tell Do not **tell** where Mother keeps the cookies.
Do not **say** where Mother keeps the cookies.

told Mary **told** me a secret.

ten **10** There are **ten** cents in a dime.

There are **10** cents in a dime.

one	two	three	four	five	six	seven	eight	nine	**ten**	eleven	twelve
1	2	3	4	5	6	7	8	9	**10**	11	12

---

tent

This is the **tent** that we live in when we go camping.

---

terrible When the two trains hit each other, there was a **terrible** wreck. It made everyone afraid.

And last of all an Admiral came,
A terrible man with a terrible name,—
A name which you all know by sight
very well,
But which no one can speak, and no one
can spell.

---

than Jim is taller **than** Bill. The rabbit can run faster than the turtle.

thank When someone does something for you, you say, "**Thank you.**" When someone gives you something, you say, "Thank you." We always thank people when they do nice things for us. We write thank you letters for our Christmas gifts.

---

thankful

When I am **thankful**, I am glad and feel like saying "Thank you."

---

thanks When we say "**Thanks,**" we mean, "**Thank you.**"
To give **thanks** means to say "Thank you."

Thanksgiving **Thanksgiving Day** comes in the month of November. Thanksgiving is the day when we give thanks for many good things.

---

that This is my book, and **that** is your book.
Do you see **that** tree across the street?
Irene said **that** she wanted to go home.
This is the house **that** Jack built.

---

the I don't want just a dog. I want **the** dog we saw in the store. The dog we saw was brown with white spots. The other dogs were not as nice as the brown one.

their

Father and I went to the Joneses' farm.

We went to see **their** horses.

We went to see the horses **that belong to them.**

---

theirs My sister and I play with Mary and her brother Jim.

These toys are ours, and the other toys are **theirs.**

These toys are ours, and the other toys **belong to them.**

---

them Your toys are new. Take care of **them.** You will want to play with them for a long time.

---

themselves The boys **themselves** said we should not go.

The children got **themselves** wet playing in the water.

Dick and Tom were playing **by themselves** away from the others.

Dick and Tom were playing **alone** away from the others.

---

then When Mother calls, **then I** will go home.

When Mother calls, **at that time** I will go home.

First we will go to the movies; **then** we will have some ice cream.

First we will go to the movies; **afterward** we will have some ice cream.

there

You sit **there** while I go into the store.

You sit **in that place** while I go into the store.

I like to go to the park. Have you ever been **there?**

Have you ever been **to that place?**

There were six candles on my birthday cake.

When I hurt myself, Mother says, "**There,** there, I'll kiss it and make it well."

---

there's **There's** means **there is.** I wonder where there's another chair.

---

these Those apples are yours, but **these** are mine.

All **these** children are my friends.

---

they The dogs have not eaten today, so **they** are hungry. Tom and Bill have been running, so they are very hot.

Mother said, "**They** say we're going to have a hot summer."

Mother said, "**People** say we're going to have a hot summer."

---

thick

This wall is **thick.**

This wall is **not thin.**

The grass is tall and **thick** in the empty lot.

The grass is tall and **growing close together** in the empty lot.

thief A person who steals is a **thief.**

Taffy was a Welshman, Taffy was a thief,
Taffy came to my house and stole a piece
of beef.
I went to Taffy's house, Taffy was
not home;
Taffy came to my house and
stole a marrow bone.

---

thieves Several **thieves** stole the money, but just one thief was caught.

---

thimble I put a **thimble** over the end of my finger when I sew. I push the needle with that finger. The thimble keeps the needle from sticking my finger.

---

thin A piece of paper is **thin.** A wall is thick.

The grass was **thin** on the side of the hill.

The grass was **growing far apart** on the side of the hill.

This dog is **thin.**

This dog is fat.

thing

What is that **thing** in the box?

These are **things** that Baby plays with.

It's a good **thing** I got to school on time.

He had his **things** in his suitcase.

He had his **clothes** in his suitcase.

---

think I **think** with my mind. I must think about what to give my mother for Christmas.

I **think** I know where my dog is hiding.

I **believe** I know where my dog is hiding.

"Really, now you ask me," said Alice, "I don't think—"

"Then you shouldn't talk," said the Hatter.

thought I **thought** of a story that my uncle used to tell me.

---

third

first	second	**third**	fourth	fifth
1st	2nd	**3rd**	4th	5th

The horse with the red blanket is third in line.

There are two horses before him.

---

thirsty I am **thirsty.** I want a drink of water.

thirty 30 There are **thirty** days in September.

There are **30** days in September.

ten	twenty	**thirty**	forty	fifty	sixty
10	20	**30**	40	50	60

---

this That apple is yours, but **this** one is mine.

Nancy will be six years old **this** week.

This man is my father.

---

those That is his toy, but **those** toys are mine.

Do you see **those** children over there? They are having a party.

---

though My plant will not grow, **though** I water it every day.

My plant will not grow, **even if** I water it every day.

---

thought I **thought** of a story that my uncle used to tell me. It just came into my mind.

I **thought** I heard a noise.

I **believed** I heard a noise.

---

thousand Ten times one hundred is one **thousand.**

Ten times 100 is **1,000.**

Fifteen thousand people live in our town. How many thousand people live in your town?

thread

Jane sews her dress with **thread.** She uses cotton thread in her needle.

Here is some red thread.

Can you **thread** the needle?

Can you **put thread through** the needle?

---

three 3

One	two	**three**	four	five
1	2	3	4	5

Did you ever hear the story of "The Three Little Pigs"?

One, two,
Buckle my shoe;
Three, four,
Shut the door;
Five, six,
Pick up sticks.

---

threw Ben **threw** his hat on the hook.

---

throat

My **throat** is the **front of my neck.**

The **inside of my neck** is also called my **throat.** A sore throat is a throat that hurts.

through Dad made a hole **through** a penny so that I could put a string in it.

Dad made a hole **from one side to the other of** a penny so that I could put a string in it.

I read **through** the comic strip.

I read **from beginning to end of** the comic strip.

Marjorie is **through** with her work.

Marjorie has **finished** with her work.

---

throw I **throw** a ball with my right arm. Some people throw a ball with the left arm.

threw Ben **threw** his hat on the hook.

thrown Sam was **thrown** from his bicycle when it struck a rock.

---

thumb One of your fingers is your **thumb.** It is your thickest finger. You have a thumb on each hand. Your fingers bend in two places. Your **thumbs** bend in only one place.

Jenny hurt her thumb.

thunder It is going to storm, and I hear a very loud noise from the sky. That is **thunder.** Lightning and thunder often come when we have a rain storm. We like to hear the thunder and see the lightning.

Thursday The **fifth day of the week** is **Thursday.**

On Thursday at three
Look out and you'll see
What Friday will be.

Sunday Monday Tuesday Wednesday Thursday Friday Saturday

---

tick Listen to a clock or watch. Do you hear a sound? That is the **tick.** The clock says, "Tick-tock."

---

ticket

I bought a **ticket** to the show. It is a little card I use to get into the show. When we ride on the train, we must buy a railroad ticket.

When we go to the moving picture show we must buy a ticket.

---

tickle Daddy's funny stories **tickle** me.

Daddy's funny stories **make** me **laugh.**

Mother used to **tickle** the bottom of my feet with her fingers. It felt funny.

tie Father wears a **tie** with his shirt. His tie is made of silk.

The race was a **tie.** The boys came to the end at the same time. Neither won.

I will **tie** a rope around the post to hold my boat.

tied James **tied** the horse to the fence.

tying Emily is **tying** a ribbon on the package.

---

tiger This is a **tiger.** He is a large wild animal. You may see a tiger in the zoo or at the circus.

---

tight

The coat was **tight** on Tom.

The coat was **not loose** on Tom.

Mother held me **tight** when she kissed me goodbye.

Mother held me **closely** when she kissed me goodbye.

---

till Mother told us we could play outdoors **till** it was dark.

Mother told us we could play outdoors **up to the time** it was dark.

Till means the same as **until.**

time You tell the **time** of day by looking at a watch or a clock.

A minute is a short **time.** Ten years is a long time.

It is **time** to go to sleep.

---

tin **Tin** is a metal. Many cans are made of tin. The cups we used at the picnic were made of tin.

---

tiny

Something **very small** is **tiny.** The bug was so tiny that you could hardly see it.

---

tip The **tip** of a thing is its **very end.** The tip of the arrow is in the tree.

Don't put the glass so near the edge of the table. It will **tip** over. It will **fall** over.

---

tiptoe I walked on **tiptoe** down the stairs. I walked on my toes so that no one would hear me.

---

tire

The rubber **tire** is on the wheel of the automobile. There are four wheels and four **tires** on an automobile. Daddy changed the tire on our automobile.

tired If you play a long time, you will get **tired** and will need to rest.

If you work hard for a long time, you will get tired.

---

to Go **to** the door and look out.

Go **as far as** the door and look out.

We went **to** a dog show yesterday.

Philip gave the cookie **to** Nancy.

I like **to** play outdoors. I do not like to stay in the house.

This is the belt **to** my blue coat.

This is the belt **that goes with** my blue coat.

---

toast I like **toast** and eggs for breakfast.

I will **toast** the bread.

I will **make** the bread **brown by heating** it.

---

today **Today** is the **day that is now.** Yesterday is the day before today.

Tomorrow is the day after today.

---

toe Your big **toe** is your first toe.

You have five **toes** on each foot.

Bill laughed when the puppy licked his toes.

together John and I went to the show **together.**

John and I went to the show **with each other.**

We have been friends together,
In sunshine and in shade,
Since first beneath the chestnut-tree
In infancy we played.

I sewed two pieces of cloth **together** to make a dress for my doll.

I sewed two pieces of cloth **to each other** to make a dress for my doll.

---

told Mary **told** me a secret.

Mary **said** to me a secret.

---

tomato

A **tomato** is really a fruit, but it tastes like a vegetable. Have you ever eaten a tomato right out of the garden?

---

tomatoes Jim likes **tomatoes** right out of the garden.

---

tomorrow The **day after today** is **tomorrow.** Today is the day that is now.

Yesterday is the day before today.

Never put off till tomorrow what you can do today.

tongue

Your **tongue** is in your mouth. You taste with your tongue. You use your tongue in speaking. You lick an envelope with your tongue.

---

tonight The **night of today** is **tonight.** Today we do not go to school, and tonight we are going to a movie.

---

too Jerry has a ball. Baby has a ball, **too.**

Baby has a ball, **also.**

This hat is **too** big for me.

This hat is **more than** big **enough** for me.

---

took I **took** my mother's hand to cross the street.

I **got hold of** my mother's hand to cross the street.

Daddy **took** us to the ball game.

Daddy **went with** us to the ball game.

Anne **took** a book from the shelf.

Anne **got** a book from the shelf.

I **took** five minutes to get ready.

I **needed** five minutes to get ready.

We **took** a bus to go downtown.

We **rode on** a bus to go downtown.

Robert **took** a package to his mother.

Robert **carried** a package to his mother.

tool

Each of these is a **tool** for doing work. We use **tools** to build things and to make things.

---

tooth

Each of my teeth is called a **tooth.**

Bob's front tooth has come out.

---

top The **top** is the **highest part of anything.** We walked from the valley to the top of the hill.

The **top** of this box is on.

The top of this box is off.

The monkey is **on top of** the dog. The dog is on the top of the horse.

This is a **top** that you spin around and around. It is a toy.

tore Harry **tore** his pants on the nail.

Harry **made a hole by pulling** his pants on the nail.

I **tore** the paper into two pieces.

I **pulled** the paper **apart** into two pieces.

---

torn Betty's skirt is **torn** where she caught it in the car door.

---

toss I will **toss** the pillow to you.

I will **throw** the pillow to you.

tossed Father **tossed** Baby up in the air.

tossing We were **tossing** the ball around.

---

touch

I will **touch** the ice.

I will **put my finger on** the ice.

touched The ice felt cold when I **touched** it.

---

toward I am going **toward** the park. If I keep on going the way I am, I will get to the park.

---

towards **Towards** means **toward.**

towel

I take a bath and then dry myself with a **towel.** I use a towel to dry dishes.

A bath **towel.**

A dish towel.

---

tower The tall, narrow part of this building is a **tower.** It is a church tower.

---

town A **town** is a **small city.** We do not live in a town; we live in the country.

---

toy Grandmother gave me a **toy.**
Grandmother gave me a **thing to play with.**

Here are some of my **toys.**

When I was sick and lay abed,
I had two pillows at my head,
And all my toys beside me lay,
To keep me happy all the day.

track A railroad **track** is the road the trains run on. It is made of iron rails.

When an animal walks in the snow or mud, he leaves the marks of his feet. This rabbit made **tracks** in the snow.

The Indians know how to **track** animals.

The Indians know how to **follow the tracks** of animals.

---

tractor

A **tractor** is a big machine that can pull heavy things. The farmer uses his tractor to pull his plow and do other work on the farm.

---

trade I will **trade** books with you. I will give you my book if you will give me your book.

We **trade with** Mr. Johnson.

We **buy from** Mr. Johnson.

---

trailer

I saw a car with a **trailer** on it. The trailer was like a room on wheels. People could sleep in it at night.

Some **trailers** are used to carry loads.

train

This is a **train** that carries people.

This is a train that carries freight.

---

trap

We use a **trap** to catch animals. Here is a fox trap.

---

travel I like to **travel.**

I like to **go from one place to another.** I like to travel by airplane.

And the Bellman, perplexed and distressed,
Said he *had* hoped, at least, when the wind blew due East,
That the ship would *not* travel due West!

---

treat Mother took us to the circus for a **treat.** Another treat was the lemonade and peanuts we had to eat.

I'll **treat** you to a bottle of pop.

I'll **buy** you a bottle of pop **for a present.**

You must always **treat** your pets well.

You must always **act** well **toward** your pets.

treated My aunt **treated** me like a big boy when she came to see us.

tree A **tree** is a very big plant. The tree trunk is wood. A tree has branches and leaves. There are many kinds of **trees.** Some are green only in summer. Some are green all the year round.

Here are three trees. Can you point to the young tree? Can you point to the live tree? Can you point to the dead tree.

Up into the cherry tree
Who should climb but little Me?

---

trick We put on false faces and played a **trick** on Bill. He did not know who we were.

My dog can do lots of **tricks.**

He sits up and begs.

He catches a ball.

He plays dead dog.

Can your dog do tricks?

---

tried I **tried** to ride my bicycle up the hill, but it was too steep.

I **tried** the cake, and it was good.

trim We will **trim** the Christmas tree. We will make it look pretty with lights and shiny balls and strips of silver paper.

Bill can **trim** his dog's hair.
Bill can **cut a little off** his dog's hair.

trimmed Father has his hair **trimmed** every two weeks.

trimming Mother is **trimming** my dress with white lace.

White lace is a good **trimming** for a dress.

---

trip To **take a trip** is to **go to a place away from home.** We are all going on an automobile trip.

Did you **trip?**
Did you **catch your foot in something and start to fall?**

tripped

Mary **tripped** on the edge of the rug, but she did not fall down.

Beth tripped over the toy wagon and fell.

---

trouble Kitty causes **trouble** when she upsets the sewing basket.

Kitty causes **extra work** when she upsets the sewing basket.

If you are naughty, you may get into **trouble.** Something that is not pleasant may happen to you.

trousers

Bob has a new pair of **trousers.**

Bob has a new pair of **pants.**

---

truck Daddy has a new **truck.** A truck is a big automobile that is made to carry a load. The farmer's potatoes are carried to market in **trucks.** Mail trucks carry the mail from the mailbox to the post office. Some trucks carry oil or gasoline in a large tank.

---

true It is **true** that two and two are four. It is true that the world is round. It is true that the sun rises in the east. Anything that is true is not a lie.

A child should always say what's true
And speak when he is spoken to.

---

trunk

A big box to put your clothes in is a **trunk.**

The lower part of a tree is called a **trunk.** A tree trunk is wood.

An elephant's long nose is called a **trunk.**

trust I **trust** you. I believe that you are honest. I believe that you will do as you say.

---

truth Always tell the **truth.**

Always tell **things that are true.**

---

try I **try** to be a good child. I will try to remember everything in my lesson.

Why don't you **try** the book and see if you like it?

tried I **tried** to ride my bicycle down the hill, but it was too steep.

trying Jim is **trying** to get his work done early so that he can go to the show.

---

tub

This is a bath **tub.**

These are wash **tubs.**

Tuesday **Tuesday** is the **third day of the week.**

Sunday Monday Tuesday Wednesday Thursday Friday Saturday

Monday's child is fair of face,
Tuesday's child is full of grace.

tulip

A **tulip** is a flower. It blooms in the spring. These are **tulips**.

---

tumble Baby's **tumble** off the chair made him cry.

Baby's **fall** off the chair made him cry.

When we're playing at the farm, we **tumble** in the hay.

When we're playing at the farm, we **bounce around** in the hay.

Ring-a-ring-a roses,
A pocket full of posies;
Hush! Hush! Hush!
We'll all tumble down.

---

tunnel We made a **tunnel** in the deep snow. A railroad often goes through a tunnel.

---

turkey

A **turkey** is a large bird. There are two in this picture. We like to eat turkey when Mother roasts it. We have turkey for Thanksgiving dinner.

turn It is my **turn** to play with the doll. When I am through, then it will be my sister's turn.

I will **turn** around and look at you.

The wheels of my wagon **turn** around and around.

The weatherman says it will **turn** cold.
The weatherman says it will **become** cold.

Turn off the cold water, and turn on the hot water.

turned My father **turned** the car around.

turning Joan is **turning** the pages of the book.

---

turnip

A **turnip** is a vegetable that grows in the garden. The part of the turnip that we eat is the root. Here are **turnips** we have gathered for cooking.

---

turtle

We saw a **turtle** walking by the side of the road. We saw another turtle turned on his back. A turtle has a hard shell on his back. Have you ever had a small turtle for a pet?

---

twelve 12 Two four six eight ten **twelve**

2 4 6 8 10 **12**

A dozen eggs is twelve eggs.

twenty 20 five ten fifteen **twenty** twenty-five thirty
5 10 15 **20** 25 30

Every lady in this land
Has twenty nails, upon each hand
Five, and twenty on hands and feet:
All this is true, without deceit.

---

twenty-five 25 twenty **twenty-five** thirty
20 **25** 30

There are twenty-five cents in a quarter.

---

twice I am **twice** as old as Mary.

I am **two times** as old as Mary. I am eight years old. Mary is four years old.

I brush my teeth **twice** every day, once in the morning and once at night.

---

twin

Margaret

Alice

Alice is my **twin.** My sister Alice and I were born on the same day. Everybody that sees us says that we are **twins** because we look alike. We wear different collars on our dresses so our teachers can tell us apart.

twinkle The stars **twinkle** at night.

Twinkle, twinkle little star,
How I wonder what you are;
Up above the world so high,
Like a diamond in the sky.

---

two 2 one **two** three four five six seven eight nine ten eleven twelve
1 2 3 4 5 6 7 8 9 10 11 12

There were two birds sat on a stone,
One flew away and then there was one,
The other bird flew after,
And then there was none,
And so the stone
Was left alone.

---

tying Emily is **tying** a ribbon in her hair.

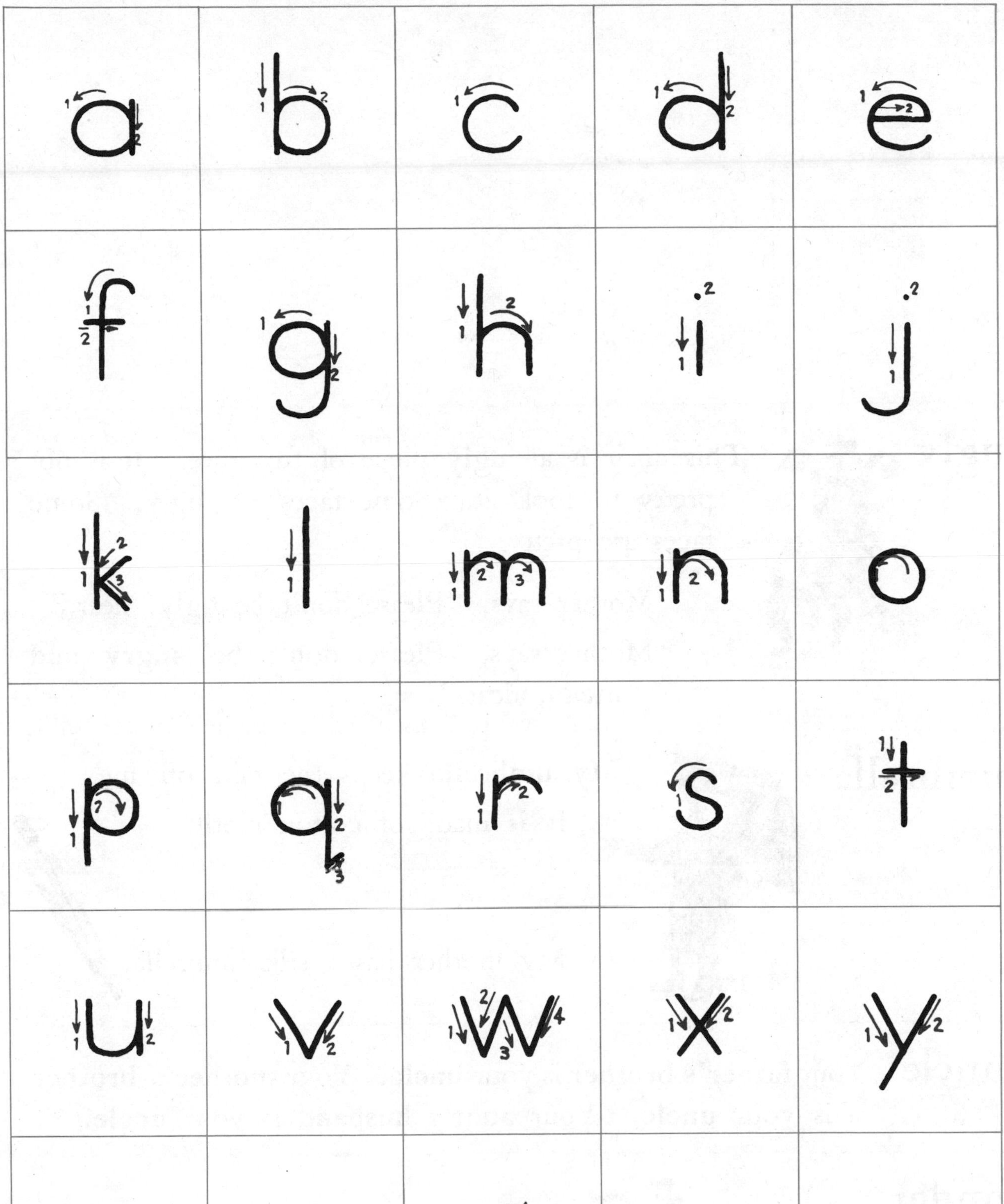

a	b	c	d	e
f	g	h	i	j
k	l	m	n	o
p	q	r	s	t
u	v	w	x	y
		z		

U u

ugly

This chair is an **ugly** piece of furniture. It is not pretty to look at. Some faces are ugly. Some faces are pretty.

Mother says, "Please don't be **ugly,** dear."

Mother says, "Please don't be **angry and mean,** dear."

umbrella

My **umbrella** keeps the rain off me. It is made of cotton cloth.

My mother has a silk umbrella.

uncle Your **father's brother** is your **uncle.** Your **mother's brother** is your **uncle.** Your **aunt's husband** is your **uncle.**

under

The dog runs **under** the fence.

The dog runs **beneath** the fence.

understand I do not **understand** how my radio works.
I do not **know** how my radio works.

understood Paul **understood** the story his mother read to him.

---

undress I will **undress** for my bath.
I will **take off my clothes** for my bath.

---

unhappy I am very **unhappy** because my dog died.
I am very **sad** because my dog died.
Sometimes when I am unhappy, I cry.

---

uniform Soldiers and sailors wear a **uniform.** Policemen wear **uniforms**, too.

United Nations

The **United Nations** is a group of many countries. It is working to stop wars and make people safe all over the world.

United States The **United States** is **our country.** There are fifty states in the United States. The flag of the United States is red, white, and blue.

Alaska
Canada
U.S.A.
Mexico
Hawaii

I pledge allegiance to the flag of the United States of America,
And to the Republic for which it stands,
One Nation, under God, indivisible,
With liberty and justice for all.

unless I will come to your house **unless** my mother says no.
I will come to your house **if** my mother does **not** say no.

---

untie When I put my shoes on, I tie my shoelaces. When I take my shoes off, I **untie** my shoelaces.

---

until I will stay here **until** Mother calls me.
I will stay here **up to the time** Mother calls me.

---

up I saw an airplane **up** in the sky.
It was far above me.

We walked **up** the hill.
We walked **to a higher part of** the hill.

---

upon

My kitty is sitting **upon** the chair.
My kitty is sitting **on** the chair.

---

upstairs My bedroom is **upstairs.**
My bedroom is **on a higher floor.**

I chased my dog **upstairs.**
I chased my dog **up the stairs.**

us Us means **myself and somebody else.** Me means myself alone. My brother, my sister, and I were trimming the Christmas tree. Mother helped us.

---

use What is the **use** of crying about it? It won't do you any good.

I **use** my arms for throwing a ball. I use my legs for running. I use my eyes for seeing.

used I **used** my toy shovel to dig in the sand.

Grace is **used to** her big bed. She has slept in it so often that it is not strange to her.

I **used to** live in the country, but now I don't.

The paint is all **used up.** There is none left.

---

useful This book is **useful.** I learn many things from it. My pen and pencil are useful. I write with them. My rubbers are useful. They keep my feet dry in wet weather.

A	B	C	D	E
F	G	H	I	J
K	L	M	N	O
P	Q	R	S	T
U	V	W	X	Y
		Z		

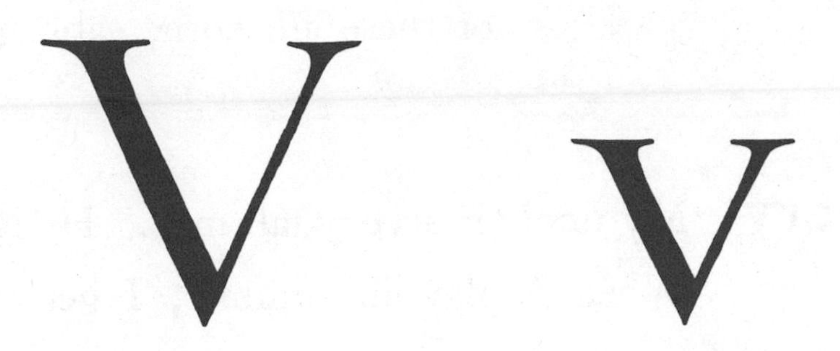

vacation A child's **vacation** is the **time he does not go to school.** We will visit Grandmother during Christmas vacation.

A grown-up's **vacation** is the **time he does not work.** Our whole family will go on a trip during my dad's vacation.

---

valentine We send letters and cards to our friends on Saint Valentine's Day. Each of these is a **valentine.** Which of these **valentines** do you like best?

---

valley

The **valley** is the **land between the hills.**

On goes the river
And out past the mill,
Away down the valley,
Away down the hill.

vegetable A **vegetable** is a plant that is used for food. A potato is a vegetable. People eat many **vegetables.** Some of these are corn, cabbage, beans, carrots, and beets.

---

very My uncle is a **very** tall man. He is much taller than most men. When I play in summer, I get very hot and very tired.

---

village

A **village** is a **small town.** There are only a few houses in the village where Mary lives.

---

vine A plant that grows along the ground is a **vine.** A plant that climbs up a wall or a tree is a vine. A pumpkin vine grows on the ground. A grape vine grows on the wall.

---

violet

This flower is a **violet.** It grows in the woods.

A violet by a mossy stone
Half hidden from the eye!
Fair as a star when only one
Is shining in the sky.

Violet is a color like purple. My mother has a pretty violet dress. The color of it is like the flower.

violin You can make music on a **violin.** Martha played on her violin.

---

visit I am going to **visit** my grandmother.

I am going to **stay for a while** with my grandmother.

---

visitor When you visit someone, you are a **visitor.** We had a visitor at our house today. My mother and I were **visitors** at my aunt's last week.

---

voice The sound I make with my mouth is my **voice.** I talk with my voice. I sing with my voice. I yell with my voice.

a	b	c	d	e
f	g	h	i	j
k	l	m	n	o
p	q	r	s	t
u	v	w	x	y
		z		

wade

I like to **wade.**
I like to **walk in the water.**

wag

My dog will **wag** his tail when he is happy.
My dog will **move** his tail **from side to side** when he is happy.

wagged When I said, "Hello, Spot," my dog **wagged** his tail and stopped barking.

wagon

I have a little **wagon.** Daddy has a big wagon. Both of our **wagons** have four wheels.

waist The part of your body that you put your belt around is your **waist.**

The **waist** of Betty's dress is white; the skirt is yellow.

---

wait Did you have a long **wait?**

Did you have a long **time to wait?**

Please **wait** for me at the street corner. Stay there until I come.

I will **wait** till Baby wakes up before I turn on the radio.

My sister and I **wait** on my mother when she is sick. We do everything she can't do for herself.

waited Bobby **waited** for his father to come home.

waiting There were many people **waiting** at the corner to get on the bus.

---

wake Daddy will **wake** when the alarm clock rings.

Daddy will **stop sleeping** when the alarm clock rings.

Let's **wake** the dog so that he can go on the picnic with us.

Let's **make** the dog **stop sleeping** so that he can go on the picnic with us.

woke I **woke** when Mother came into my room.

I woke before the morning, I was happy all the day,
I never said an ugly word, but smiled and stuck to play.

walk Mother and I will **take a walk.**

Mother and I will **go walking.**

When I walk, **I take one step after another with my feet.** Some animals walk; some crawl. A dog will walk. A snake will crawl.

walked Jim **walked** through the fields and woods.

walking Jim likes to go **walking** with his dog.

---

wall On the **wall** of my bedroom there is a picture of a sail boat.

The rose bushes grow along the **wall** in our back yard.

Humpty-Dumpty sat on a wall,
Humpty-Dumpty had a great fall;
All the king's horses and all the king's men
Couldn't put Humpty-Dumpty together again.

---

want I **want** a big red apple.

I **would like to have** a big red apple.

I **want** a new pair of shoes.

I **need** a new pair of shoes.

wanted Our dog **wanted** to go into the house.

wants Mother **wants** us to go to sleep.

war A **war** is a **fight between countries.** The army fights in a war on land. The navy fights in a war on the sea.

---

warm

When I stand near the fire, I am **warm.** When I stand too near the fire, I am hot.

It is **warm** in the sunshine; it is cool in the shade of a tree.

I wear **warm** mittens in winter.

I wear mittens **that keep me warm** in winter.

---

was Jack **was** riding my bicycle yesterday. It was a long time ago that I first got my bicycle.

---

wash I **wash** my face and hands before I eat.

I **clean** my face and hands **with water** before I eat. I use soap, too.

washed

Alice has **washed** her doll's clothes.

washing Jane and her brother are **washing** the dishes.

---

wasn't **Wasn't** means **was not.** I wasn't at home yesterday.

waste We must never **waste** food.

We must never **use** food **so that a part of it will have to be thrown away.**

We must never **waste** money.

We must never **spend** money **so that we get nothing good for it.**

---

watch 

I can tell the time of day by looking at Daddy's **watch.** My mother wears a watch on her wrist.

Watch me jump over the chair.

Look at me jump over the chair.

We'll **watch** for Daddy's car to come down the street.

We'll **look for** Daddy's car to come down the street.

Watch out that you don't fall down.

Be careful that you don't fall down.

Angels will **guard** you, **watch over** you, dear,
So rock-a-bye, baby, Mother is here.

watched I **watched** for the postman to bring me a letter.

watching Jerry stood **watching** the fish swim around in the fish bowl.

---

water We drink **water.** We wash in water. The rivers and lakes and oceans are filled with water.

Mother is going to **water** her flowers.

Mother is going to **put water on** her flowers.

watermelon

A **watermelon** is a very large fruit. **Watermelons** are pink inside and full of sweet juice. They grow in the fields on vines. Do you like to eat watermelon?

---

wave

I **wave** to my father.

A **wave** on the ocean.

There is a **wave** in Mother's hair.

waved He **waved** goodbye.

waving The man was **waving** a lantern.

---

wax

Bees make **wax** and use it to build a kind of box in which to store their honey.

Mother puts **wax** on the floor. Then she rubs it to make the floor shine.

'The time has come,' the Walrus said,
'To talk of many things;
Of shoes—and ships—and sealing wax—
Of cabbages—and—kings—
And why the sea is boiling hot—
And whether pigs have wings.'

way How far is it from your house to the school? It's a long **way.**

What street do you take to Mary's house? This is the **way.**

How do you make your dog obey? I do it this **way.**

Ralph looked up and down the street. First he looked this **way,** then that way.

Jean used to wear her hair in curls. Now she wears it a new **way.**

It isn't nice to want your own **way** all the time.

---

we When I talk about **myself and some others,** I use the word **we.** When Katherine, Mary and I left home, it was raining. We had umbrellas, so we didn't get wet.

---

weak When I was sick, I was **weak** and had to stay in bed.

When I was sick, I was **not strong** and had to stay in bed.

Daddy docsn't like **weak** tea.

---

wear Polly will **wear** her new dress at the party.

Polly will **have on** her new dress at the party.

wearing My doll is **wearing** her red dress now.

wore It was snowing outside, so I **wore** my boots.

worn Laura has **worn** her red coat all winter.

weather The **weather** is warm today.

The **air outdoors** is warm today.

It is raining and cold, and the wind is blowing. The weather is bad.

The sun is shining, and the sky is clear. The weather is good.

Wednesday The **fourth day of the week** is **Wednesday.**

Sunday Monday Tuesday Wednesday Thursday Friday Saturday

---

wee It was just a **wee** flower.

It was just a **tiny** flower.

She is a winsome wee thing,
She is a handsome wee thing,
She is a bonnie wee thing,
This sweet wee wife o' mine.

---

week A **week** is made up of **seven days.** The days of a week are Sunday, Monday, Tuesday, Wednesday, Thursday, Friday, and Saturday. There are four **weeks** in a month. There are fifty-two weeks in a year.

weigh

To **weigh** is to **measure how heavy a thing is.** I weigh fifty pounds.

---

weight How heavy are you? What is your **weight?** Your weight is measured in pounds. David's weight is fifty-three pounds.

---

welcome You are always **welcome** here. We are always glad to have you.

When someone says, "Thank you," you say, "You're **welcome.**"

---

well Are you **well** today?

Are you **in good health** today?

Bess plays the piano **well.** She is good at playing the piano.

Sometimes when we start to say something, we say, "Oh, **well.**"

At the farm we get water from a **well.**

At the farm we get water from a **deep hole in the ground.**

---

we'll A short way to write and say **we will** is **we'll.** I hope we'll see you again soon.

went The boy **went** very fast on his bicycle.

The boy **moved forward** very fast on his bicycle.

The clock **went** as long as it was wound every day.

The clock **ran** as long as it was wound every day.

Joe **went** to his grandfather's farm yesterday morning. He came home last night.

The path **went** to the swimming pool.

Do you remember how that poem **went?**

---

were Kate, Jill, and Bobby **were** playing with my toys yesterday.

Mother and Father were married ten years ago.

---

we're **We're** means **we are.** I think we're the first ones here.

---

west

If you look at the sun as it goes down in the evening, you will be looking **west.** West is to your left on a map when you read it.

Three geese in a flock,
One flew east, one flew west,
And one flew over the goose's nest.

---

wet My dog swam in the lake and got **wet.**

He does not like to be wet.

I will dry him with a towel.

what Do you know **what** makes a clock tick? What is the answer to this question? I don't know what the answer is.

---

what's **What's** means **what is.** What's Baby crying about?

---

wheat You can see **wheat** growing in the field. The grains of wheat are ground into flour, and the flour is made into bread.

---

wheel 

A **wheel** is round. There are **wheels** on a wagon. A bicycle has two wheels. An automobile has four wheels. The wheel came off my toy carriage.

Sometimes a **bicycle** is called a **wheel.**

---

when Do you know **when** Mother will be home?
Do you know **at what time** Mother will be home?

---

whenever I will meet you **whenever** you tell me to.
I will meet you **at any time** you tell me to.

---

where **Where** do you live?
In what place do you live?

Where, oh, where has my little dog gone?
Where, oh, where can he be?
With his ears cut short and his tail cut long—
Oh, where, oh, where can he be?

whether I don't know **whether** to put a red dress or a blue dress on my doll.

I don't know which of the two dresses to choose.

I must go to school **whether** it rains or not.

---

which That is the story **which** our teacher read to us.

Which one of the hats is yours?

If you could travel by train or airplane which one would you choose? Which way would you rather go?

---

while I will work **while** you play.

I will work **at the same time** that you play.

Pat waited a **while** for his father to come.

Pat waited a **time** for his father to come.

---

whip

The man that rode the horse carried a **whip.**

If he needed to, he would **whip** the horse lightly.

If he needed to, he would **strike** the horse lightly **with his whip.**

whisper Mother spoke to me in a **whisper.**

Mother spoke to me in a **very soft voice.**

I **whisper** when I don't want to wake the baby.

whispered  I **whispered** to Bob about our secret.

---

whistle  I can **whistle.** Can you?

This is a whistle. When you blow on it, it makes a loud noise. 

---

white **White** is a color. Many people of the world have a skin color from pinkish white to brown. They are called **white** people.

Over the river and through the wood
To grandfather's house we'll go;
The horse knows the way
To carry the sleigh,
Through the white and drifted snow.

---

who **Who** is this boy beside us? Who are those children over there?

This is the friend **who** went with me. And these are the others who stayed home.

whole The **whole** of anything is **all** of it.

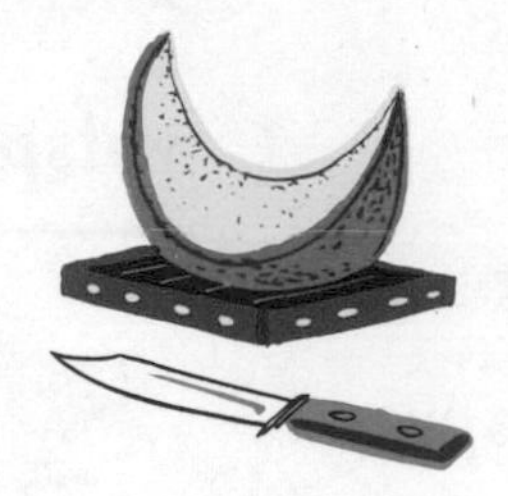

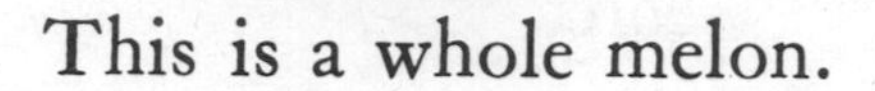

This is a whole melon. This is a part of the melon.

---

whom The girl to **whom** I waved is my best friend.

---

whose **Whose** dog is this? To whom does he belong?

---

why Do you know **why** it is so cold today?
Do you know **the reason that** it is so cold today?

---

wide The horse went into the barn through a **wide** door. It was not narrow.

I measured my sheet of paper. It was ten inches long and eight inches **wide.**

---

wife A **married woman** is a **wife.** A married man is a husband. My mother is my father's wife. Bob says that when he grows up, he will be married and have a wife.

wild

The **wild** animals live in the fields and woods. They run away and hide when you go near them. A cat is a tame animal that lives in the house. A wildcat is a wild animal.

Mother says, "Sometimes the children are too **wild.** They run and shout too much."

The wind tonight is **wild.** It is as strong and fierce as a tiger.

---

will I **will** come to see you tomorrow. My aunt will visit us for a week. Jane will take her baby brother for a walk after his nap.

would Susan **would** like to go to the show. Would you go with her?

I **would** help you if I could.

---

willow

A **willow** tree grows near our house.

---

win To win you must **do better than anyone else who is trying to do the same thing.** I hope Jack will win the race.

won Jack **won** the race.

wind Can you **wind** the string into a ball?
Can you **turn** the string **around** into a ball?

---

wind

Wind is **air moving.** When the wind blew hard, I lost my hat.

O wind, a-blowing all day long,
O wind, that sings so loud a song.

---

windy It is a **windy** day.
It is a day **full of wind.**

---

window I looked out of the **window** at the snow falling. We must keep the **windows** closed in cold weather.

---

wing

A bird's **wing** is covered with feathers. A bird moves his two **wings** when he flies through the air. The wings are to fly with.

The **wings** of an airplane hold it up in the air.

winter

Winter is **one of the four seasons** of the year. Autumn, spring, and summer are the other seasons. In some parts of our country there is snow in the winter.

> Cold and raw the north winds blow,
> Bleak in the morning early;
> All the hills are covered with snow,
> And winter's now come fairly.

---

wipe

When I wash my face, I **wipe** it with a towel. When I wash my face, I **rub** it **dry** with a towel. I wipe my muddy feet before I come into the house. I wipe the dishes after Bill washes them.

---

wire

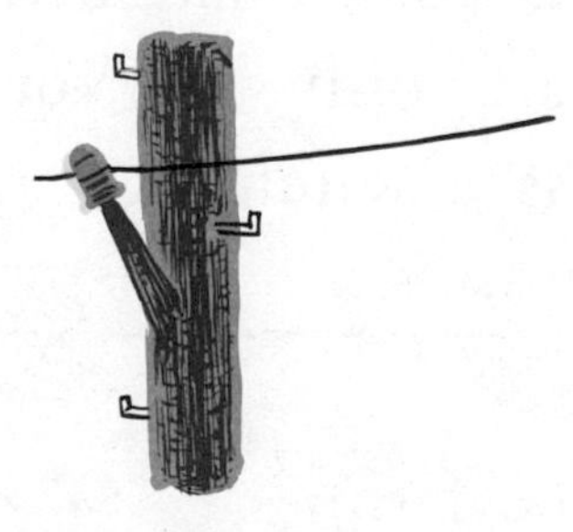

Telephone **wire.**

A wire fence.

Electric wire.

---

wise My father is a **wise** man. He knows about many things.

wish You can make a **wish** on the first star you see at night.

Star light, star bright,
First star I've seen tonight,
Wish I may, wish I might
Get the wish I wish tonight.

I **wish** it were Christmas Day.
I **want** it to be Christmas Day.

I **wish you** a happy birthday.
I **hope you have** a happy birthday.

wished Tommy **wished** to be a clown in a circus.

wishing I was **wishing** that Mother would come to help me.

---

wishes Mary made three **wishes.**

---

witch

Have you heard stories about a fairy, an elf, or a **witch?** These are all people of the Land of Make Believe. They are only in stories. This is a witch.

---

with I am going **with** my daddy to the farm.

I like my new dress **with** the lace trimming.

We eat **with** a knife, a fork, and a spoon.

My teacher is pleased **with** my good work.

within I will be there **within** a half hour.

I will be there **in not more than** a half hour.

---

without

Richard ran out **without** a hat.

Richard ran out **with no** hat.

---

woke I **woke** when Mother came into my room.

I woke before the morning, I was happy all the day.
I never said an ugly word, but smiled and stuck to **play.**

---

wolf

A **wolf** is a wild animal. It looks like a big dog.

---

wolves There are still some **wolves** in the west part of the United States.

---

woman My mother is a **woman.** My daddy is a man. A girl grows up to be a **woman.**

---

women There were several **women** at the party.

won Jack **won** the race.

Jack **did better than anyone else** in the race.

---

wonder I **wonder** what is wrong with my toy train.

I ask myself what is wrong with my toy train. It will not run.

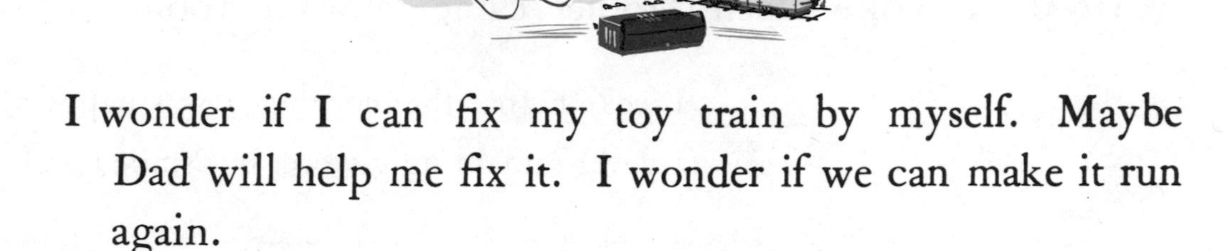

I wonder if I can fix my toy train by myself. Maybe Dad will help me fix it. I wonder if we can make it run again.

No wonder Baby can't talk; she's too young.

It is not a surprise that Baby can't talk; she's too young.

---

wonderful It was **wonderful** to see the country from an airplane. It is wonderful to look at a city from a very tall building.

Great wide, beautiful, wonderful world,
With the wonderful waters round you curled,
And the wonderful grass upon your breast,
World, you are beautifully dressed.

---

won't **Will not** and **won't** mean the same thing. Don won't let the dog sleep on his bed.

wood We cut down trees and saw them up to get **wood.** Wood is used in many ways.

Here are some things made of wood.

---

woods Many trees growing near each other made the **woods.** The woods were cool and shady, and the birds were singing.

---

wooden Did you ever see a pair of **wooden** shoes?
Did you ever see a pair of shoes **made of wood?**

---

woodpecker

This bird is called a **woodpecker.** A woodpecker pecks holes in tree trunks. He pecks the holes to get bugs to eat.

---

wool **Wool** is the **fur that grows on sheep.** The sheep's wool is cut off and made into wool cloth. The wool cloth is then made into clothes, blankets, and other things. When Bobby goes out to play in winter, he wears a wool snow suit.

woolen **Woolen** means **made of wool.**

---

word Each **word** in this book is explained. We use **words** to talk with. You use words when you write. When you read, you know what the words mean.

---

wore

It was snowing outside, so I **wore** my boots.

---

work My **work** is to help clean the house.

I like to **work.** When I do not work, I play or rest.

worked I **worked** all morning cutting the grass.

working My daddy is not **working** today. He is resting.

works My sister **works** after school delivering newspapers.

---

world

The **whole earth and the sky** is the **world.** This is a picture of the world.

---

worm A **worm** moves by crawling. When it rains in the spring, the **worms** come out of the ground. We dug up some worms to use for our fishing trip. We put them in a can.

worn Laura is wearing a red coat. She has **worn** it all winter.

My shoes are nearly **worn out.** When anything is used for a long time, it may become worn out.

---

worry My dog is sick. I **worry** about whether he will get well.

I am unhappy wondering whether he will get well.

---

worse My dog has been sick; he is **worse** today.

My dog has been sick; he is **more sick** today.

My kitty was bad, but yours acted **worse.**

My kitty was bad, but yours acted **more badly.**

---

worth Mother bought a dollar's **worth** of meat. The meat cost a dollar.

That book is not **worth** reading.

That book is not **good enough for** reading.

This toy is **worth** one dollar. It cost one dollar.

would Susan **would** like to go to the show. **Would** you go with her?

I **would** help you if I could.

---

wouldn't **Would not** and **wouldn't** mean the same. John wouldn't let me ride in his wagon.

---

wrap

To **wrap** is to **put a covering around.** I will wrap your box in paper.

wrapped Ben **wrapped** himself in a blanket and lay on the ground.

---

wraps Put on your **wraps** before you go outdoors.

Put on your **coat and hat** before you go outdoors.

---

wreck

This is an automobile **wreck.**

Don't **wreck** my house of blocks.

Don't **break up** my house of blocks.

---

wren A little **wren** sat on a branch outside my window. It was a little bird singing a loud, sweet song.

wrist

My **wrist** is between my hand and my lower arm. I can turn my hand on my wrist. Mother wears a watch around her wrist.

---

write You **write** when you make letters and words on paper. Sometimes you write with a pencil. Sometimes you write with a pen. Can you write your name?

writing I am **writing** a letter to my uncle.

written I have **written** a story about my cat and her kittens.

wrote I **wrote** my name ten times.

---

wrong

I put my gloves on the **wrong** hands. They are not on right.

It is **wrong** to lie. It is right to tell the truth.

---

wrote I **wrote** my name ten times.

a	*b*	*c*	*d*	*e*
f	*g*	*h*	*i*	*j*
k	*l*	*m*	*n*	*o*
p	*q*	*r*	*s*	*t*
u	*v*	*w*	*x*	*y*
		z		

X is a **letter** we use in ax, box, ox, fox.

ax

box

fox

ox

1	2	3
4	5	6
7	8	9
	10	

Y y

yard

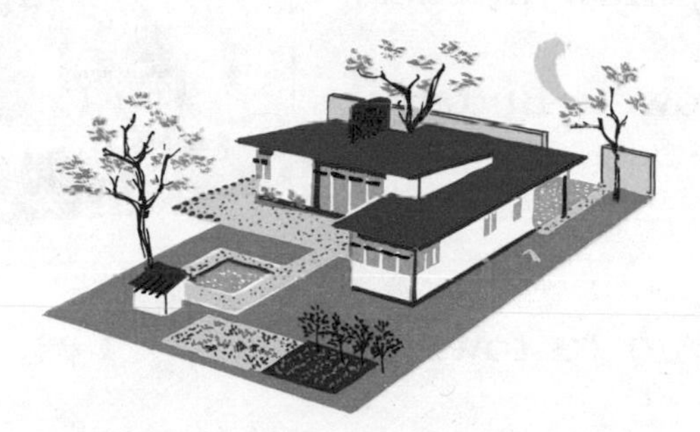

The **ground around our house** is the **yard.** Grass and flowers grow in our yard.

1 yard = 3 feet.

A yard of string is a piece of string three feet long.

yarn

Wool is sometimes made into **yarn.**
Wool is sometimes made into **long threads.**
Cotton and silk are also made into yarn.

Mother is making a sweater with wool yarn.

year There are **twelve months** in a **year.** They are January, February, March, April, May, June, July, August, September, October, November, and December. I am five **years** old. My brother is seven years old.

yell

The puppy let out a **yell** when his tail was stepped on.

The puppy let out a **loud cry** when his tail was stepped on.

I like to **yell** at the ball game.

---

yellow yellow This is the color **yellow.**

How do you like my yellow pitcher?

Many flowers are yellow. Butter is yellow.

---

yes Daddy asked if I wanted to go to town. I said, **"Yes, I do."**

When the children asked me to play, I didn't know whether to say yes or no.

---

yesterday The **day before today** is **yesterday.** Today is the day that is now.

Tomorrow is the day after today.

---

yet I haven't combed my hair **yet.**

I haven't combed my hair **up till now.**

Don't take off your coat **yet.**

Don't take off your coat **this soon.**

That dog is barking **yet.**

That dog is barking **still.**

I ran as fast as I could, **yet** I could not catch him.

I ran as fast as I could, **but** I could not catch him.

you **You** can mean **one person** or **more than one person.** The teacher said to the children, "Are you all here?" Then Jane came in the room. She said, "Oh, there you are, Jane."

---

you'll **You'll** means **you will.** I think you'll like my new coat.

---

young I am **young.** Grandfather is old.

The old bird must feed the young ones.

---

your Can **your** pony run faster than mine? This is your pony; it belongs to you.

---

you're **You are** and **you're** mean the same thing. I think you're pretty.

---

yours That hat is **yours.**

That hat **belongs to you.**

---

yourself If I leave you, you will be **by yourself.**

If I leave you, you will be **alone.**

Did you stick **yourself** with the needle?

You **yourself** should keep your room neat.

A B C D E
F G H I J
K L M N O
P Q R S T
U V W X Y
Z

zebra

A **zebra** is an animal with colored stripes on his body. The zebra is about as big as a small horse.

zero **Zero** means **none** or **nothing**. This is called a zero: **o**.

When people say, "It's almost **zero** today," they mean that it is very cold outdoors.

zoo There are many wild and strange animals at the **zoo**.

a	b	c	d	e
f	g	h	i	j
k	l	m	n	o
p	q	r	s	t
u	v	w	x	y
		z		